The Prayers of a Builder

the apostle Paul's pattern of prayer

by John Ryan

Unless otherwise indicated, Scripture quotations taken from *The Holy Bible, New International Version*® NIV® Copyright © 1973 1978 1984 2011 by Biblica, Inc. TM Used by permission. All rights reserved worldwide.

Where indicated (NLT), Scripture quotations taken from *Holy Bible: New Living Translation.* Wheaton, Ill: Tyndale House Publishers, 2004.

Table of Contents

Introduction

The world, and the Church of Jesus Christ—which is in the world, but not of it—are facing very significant change in this generation. The world is quickly moving ever closer to what the Bible foretells as a time of oppressive global government and of severe persecution against the people of God. The day may not be far off when even in the "enlightened" West, Christians could face imprisonment or worse for their commitment to Jesus Christ.

Nevertheless, Jesus promised, "I will build my church, and the gates of hell will not prevail against it." So we know that, whatever happens in this world, the Lord is continuing to fulfill this promise to us. But the edifying of the Body of Christ is a spiritual process, not a social or political one. Christians certainly have a stake in political and social developments; we are free, at least at present, to advocate our convictions and preferences in these realms. But we ought never to confuse struggles to shape this present world with the work God is doing to prepare His people for that glorious destination which far transcends this world, in which this present world will hardly be remembered.

The Bible foretells terrible developments on earth before the return of Jesus Christ. We do not look forward to these things. But they must happen, according to Scripture, and cannot be stopped. Resistance, in the sense of arresting these things and rolling them back, is futile. This does not mean, however, that the Church can do nothing but cower in a dark corner. Rather, this is the time for the Church to arise, to take hold of the Lord and His Word as never before, and to shine more and more brightly for Christ.

But, to repeat, arising and shining for God is the spiritual outcome of a spiritual process. We cannot achieve this spiritual outcome by employing the carnal power of votes, or protests, or social action. We can

1

pursue spiritual ends only through the spiritual means given to us by God, as set forth in His Word. There is no other way for the Church to arise and shine and testify for God before this increasingly dark and wicked world.

One of the mighty spiritual means God has given to His people so that we can work with Him to accomplish His purposes is prayer. That's what this book is about. My hope with this work is threefold:

1. To impart understanding of Scripture on the subject of prayer, in order to:

2. Provoke effectual, fervent prayer that is pleasing to God and that avails much, in order that He may:

3. Equip and empower the Church to edify itself in love, unto the measure of the stature of the fullness of Christ (Ephesians 4), and thus glorify the Lord.

The first thing that needs to be said about prayer is that God has ordained it and blessed it. He is sovereign over His creation and His purposes for it, yet He has invited His people to have a vital part, through prayer, in the accomplishment of His plans. The capacity we have, through prayer, to help build and extend God's Kingdom and eternally to affect the lives of others, can hardly be overstated. Sadly, we tend to underrate the importance of prayer and to live far below this amazing privilege God has given us. Praying is a mighty, essential ministry, and the wise take it seriously.

The second thing that needs to be said about prayer is that regenerated, true believers in Jesus Christ have full, unrestricted access to God's Throne of Grace in Heaven. Jesus has made a way for us, through the Cross, to approach the Father boldly with our requests and needs. The clear message of the whole book of

Hebrews is, to paraphrase, "Jesus has opened the way into the Holy of Holies for us, so let's go in! Don't be like those ancient Israelites who drew back because of unbelief and fell in the desert. Don't draw back, draw near!" In numerous other passages of Scripture, the Lord fully and freely welcomes us to come to Him by faith. If there is any constraint on our prayer lives, it lies in us, not in Him.

Being assured of these two things alone, every one of God's people can be and should be exceedingly fruitful in prayer. Apart from needing new birth and cleansing through Christ, there is no condition—neither age, nor health, nor status in the church, nor experience, nor anything else—restricting our access to God in prayer. So it is sad when Christians have little interest in or faith for effectual prayer.

Most sad of all, perhaps, are "senior saints" who feel they have been put on the shelf by God and/or their church, and that they are no longer capable of fruitful ministry. This notion of relegation to uselessness is simply false. Churches may assign seniors "to the back pasture," but God does not. Elderly saints may face diminishing human fellowship and activity, especially in these strange times, but their access to God is unlimited and their fellowship with Him need never diminish. May languishing seniors and shut-ins grasp the life-giving truth of Scripture and arise and shine for Christ through prayer. Wonderful exploits and eternal joys await those who do!

Prayer that pleases and moves God most is prayer that seeks what He desires. Jesus instructs His disciples to pray like this: "Our Father, who art in Heaven, hallowed be Thy name. Thy Kingdom come, Thy will be done." The primary purpose of prayer is not to fulfill our desires, but to bring glory to God through the fulfillment and outworking of His will, His desires. Prayer is effectual to the degree that it seeks God's glory through the accomplishment of His purposes.

It is vital then to understand, as we come to pray, what the will of God is. If we don't have a clear conception of His purposes, then how can we pray for them to be accomplished? We usually know what we want, but how can we pray in a manner that pleases the Lord if we don't know what He desires? Thankfully, in Scripture the Lord has told us, with great clarity, what His desires are. He has also given us abundant guidance, a pattern or template, for praying according to His will, that His desires may be fulfilled.

As we will see, Christ's foremost passionate desire and plan is for the edification and maturing of His Bride, the Church, into spiritual fullness and completeness in Him. And the prayer pattern that He has laid out in Scripture unerringly guides us toward fruitful participation in that plan and, simultaneously, toward our own growth, maturing and blessing.

I believe that those who are able to receive the exhortation in this volume will find their prayer lives greatly enriched. More importantly, they will find their prayer lives greatly enriching others, helping bring to individuals, to congregations, and to the whole Body of Christ the unspeakable blessing which it is continually in God's great heart to give, but for which He has adamantly determined that His people seek Him.

1. The Wellspring of Effectual Prayer

wellspring: *the head or source of a spring, stream, river, etc.; fountainhead; a source or supply of anything, especially when considered inexhaustible*

A truth of the greatest importance needs to made very clear here, at the beginning of this study. The last thing teaching on prayer should ever do is impose an unbiblical burden of compulsion or condemnation on the reader or listener. Unfortunately, for many believers, the very mention of prayer induces a soul-sapping mixture of guilt and weariness. It's a sad but understandable fact that many Christians find praying to be a tedious grind. If it were otherwise, more believers would happily be doing more praying.

Naturally enough, believers who don't find praying enjoyable tend to spend minimal time in prayer, or avoid praying altogether. And then, because they know they should pray, they condemn themselves for not praying, or not praying enough. There is something terribly wrong with this fruitless dynamic. And the likely problem at its root can affect not only our prayer lives but every aspect of our Christian walk.

What is the "root problem"? I believe it's often this: Attempting to produce fruit and good works such as prayer, while having an inadequate connection to Jesus the Vine, the one and only source of true fruitfulness. There's a subtle but very real and vital difference between trying to do good things to fulfill God's will and thereby please Him; versus drawing near to the Lord and receiving from Him the life, wisdom, grace and spiritual strength which bring forth in us the good fruit that pleases Him.

Contrary to what is probably a very common misconception, "prayer" is not the Christian's source of spiritual life, nor is it the prime necessity of his or her walk with God. Prayer is a very important part of Christian life, but it is not the most important.

What is the most important? The Lord has told us, repeatedly: In order to have spiritual life and to continue in that life, we must come to Jesus Christ and listen to Him. We come to Him by faith, believing that He is, and that He desires fellowship with us. And we listen to what He has to say to us, which He communicates through His Word, the Scriptures. He has the words of life, and we need to hear them. As we come to Him in faith and read or hear His words with receptive hearts, He speaks life to us. And that life is then manifested in us, naturally, through every sort of good fruit and good work.

I would invite you to reflect deeply on the following Bible passages, noting their emphasis on being with the Lord (coming, abiding, remaining, sitting at the Lord's feet) and hearing Him (if my words abide in you, learn from me, listen to me, listened to His teaching). Note also the absence of the word "prayer":

I am the true vine, and my Father is the vinedresser. Every branch in me that does not bear fruit he takes away, and every branch that does bear fruit he prunes, that it may bear more fruit. Already you are clean because of the word that I have spoken to you. Abide in me, and I in you. As the branch cannot bear fruit by itself, unless it abides in the vine, neither can you, unless you abide in me. I am the vine; you are the branches. Whoever abides in me and I in him, he it is that bears much fruit, for apart from me you can do nothing (John 15:1-11).

Come to me, all who labour and are heavy laden, and I will give you rest. Take my yoke upon you, and learn from me, for I am gentle and lowly in heart, and you will find rest for your souls. For my yoke is easy, and my burden is light (Matthew 11:2-3).

Now as they went on their way, Jesus entered a village. And a woman named Martha welcomed him into her house. And she had a sister called Mary, who sat at the Lord's feet and listened to his teaching. But Martha was distracted with much serving. And she went up to him and said, "Lord, do you not care that my sister has left me to serve alone? Tell her then to help me." But the Lord answered her, "Martha, Martha, you are anxious and troubled about many things, but one thing is necessary. Mary has chosen the good portion, which will not be taken away from her" (Luke 10: 38-42).

And consider this wonderful passage:

Come, everyone who thirsts, come to the waters; and he who has no money, come, buy and eat! Come, buy wine and milk without money and without price. Why do you spend your money for that which is not bread, and your labour for that which does not satisfy? Listen diligently to me, and eat what is good, and delight yourselves in rich food. Incline your ear, and come to me; hear, that your soul may live (Isaiah 55:1-3).

In these three short verses, the Lord says "come" five times, and "listen" or the equivalent three times. What is He telling us? Very clearly and simply, He's telling us "Come!" and "Listen!" As we respond in obedient faith and do this, we *will* receive abundantly and freely from the treasury of God's riches in glory. We *will* be satisfied, delighting in the unspeakable goodness of the Lord. And we *will* truly live.

The Lord goes on to say in Isaiah 55:

As the heavens are higher than the earth, so are my ways higher than your ways and my thoughts than your thoughts. As the rain and the snow come down from heaven, and do not return to it without watering the earth and making it bud and flourish, so that it yields seed for the sower and bread for the eater, so is my word that goes out from my mouth: It will not return to me empty, but will accomplish what I desire and achieve the purpose for which I sent it. You will go out in joy and be led forth in peace; the mountains and hills will burst into song before you, and all the trees of the field will clap their hands. Instead of the thornbush will grow the juniper, and instead of briers the myrtle will grow. This will be for the Lord's renown . . . (Isaiah 55:9-13).

How instructive this passage is! As we come to the Lord and receive His words, letting them "sink down into our ears" as Jesus put it in Luke 9:44, they will accomplish what He desires and achieve the purpose for which He sent them. His words are like the rain and snow which water the earth, not only refreshing all life, but causing the ground to bring forth bountiful crops. God's words do the same thing in our hearts and lives as we receive them and let them sink in.

And what is it that God desires to accomplish through speaking His words to us His people, and for what purpose has He sent them? Just this: That we may "go out in joy and be led forth in peace." When we draw near to the Lord, diligently applying our hearts to Scripture and allowing Scripture to penetrate our hearts, we will go out from that "secret place of the Most High" with joy and peace. Our lives will be filled with fruit instead of thorns and weeds. We will glorify the Lord. And our prayers also, inspired and guided by Scripture, will be fruitful, pleasing the Lord and glorifying Him.

Jesus said, "If you abide in me, and my words abide in you, ask whatever you wish, and it will be done for you. By this my Father is glorified, that you bear much fruit and so prove to be my disciples" (John 15: 7-8). Note the order: First, abide in Christ. Draw near to Him. Be with Him so that we can receive from Him what we desperately need and what only He can give. Listen to

His words. Listen carefully. He has wonderful things to teach us out of His Word, including wonderful truth about prayer. Then comes prayer, with sound, biblical understanding of what the Lord wants and how He would have us pray. And then comes fruit, as naturally as grapes appearing on a vine, bringing glory to God.

From simply coming to Jesus by faith, being with Him, devoting time and attention to Him, listening to Him through His word, and receiving from Him—as John 6 teaches, feeding on Him—we will have coursing in us the very life of God. That life will also fill our prayer life, inspiring prayer that is according to the will of God and Word of God, motivated by the love of God. Such prayer will be effectual. And, more and more, it will be a delight.

Effectual prayer does not arise from the fleshly strivings of parched souls, barely connected with the Vine. Rather, it is a fruit of "the one necessary thing"— waiting on the Lord in faith, listening carefully to what He says, and receiving the life and refreshing that come only through our connection with our friend and Lord, Jesus Christ.

If you are spiritually parched, and if the thought of prayer repels or condemns you, please consider this counsel: Do "the one necessary thing." Draw near to Jesus, by faith. Give Him time and attention, when you reasonably are able. In these times with Him, don't try to force yourself to pray. Open your Bible to John 15 and Luke 10:38-42 and Isaiah 55. Read and ponder. Read and receive. Read and understand. Trust that the Lord will never turn away those who come to Him in truth, or deny them His grace. I believe He will transform not only your prayer life, but all of your life. As Jesus said, "It is the Spirit who gives life; the flesh is no help at all. The words that I have spoken to you are Spirit and they are life" (John 6:63).

Don't let your prayer life be driven by anxiety, anger, guilt or fear. Rather, let it be the peaceable fruit of your relationship with Jesus and of the insight and guidance you receive from the Word. Let Jesus lead you, gently, into fruitful prayer inspired by His love. Let Him establish you in a life of effectual prayer that is pleasing to Him and a great blessing to others—and to you.

2. The Church of Jesus Christ Will Not Fail

The evil powers of this present world are closing in on the Church. Nearly every day brings news of some fresh attack against God's people, from brutal physical persecution in parts of Africa, to harsh government suppression in China, to social, political and legal targeting and silencing in the once-enlightened West.

At the same time, the professing Church is facing internal crises. In the US, for example, a steady procession of church leaders have been either resigning in disgrace due to exposure of gross sins, or proudly renouncing their faith in Christ. Church attendance is in decline, as is the percentage of children in Christian homes who commit to following Jesus. Many churches are abandoning scriptural principles and pursuing unbiblical "woke" agendas instead. Others are consumed with the pursuit of numerical growth, prosperity and the approval of men, at the expense of truth. Still others have turned aside from seeking God according to His word to engage in unbiblical "disciplines" and mysticism.

It seems as if that which Paul foretold is happening: "For the time is coming when people will not endure sound teaching, but having itching ears they will accumulate for themselves teachers to suit their own passions, and will turn away from listening to the truth and wander off into myths" (2 Timothy 4:3-4).

Nevertheless, no matter how much persecution and apostasy afflict the Church, we can be sure of this: The Lord will protect and keep His faithful flock from defeat. He is going to present to Himself a glorious, triumphant Bride—all the more radiant for those trials which, through His grace, she has endured and overcome.

Jesus promised, " . . . on this rock I will build my church, and the gates of hell shall not prevail against it"

11

(Matt. 16:18). His plan is to edify the Church until it reaches "the measure of the stature of the fullness of Christ" (Eph. 4:13) and to "sanctify her, having cleansed her by the washing of water with the word, so that he might present the church to himself in splendour, without spot or wrinkle or any such thing, that she might be holy and without blemish" (Eph. 5:26-27).

Psalm 46 assures God's people of our ultimate victory:

God is our refuge and strength,a very present help in trouble.Therefore we will not fear though the earth gives way, though the mountains be moved into the heart of the sea, though its waters roar and foam, though the mountains tremble at its swelling. There is a river whose streams make glad the city of God, the holy habitation of the Most High. God is in the midst of her; she shall not be moved; God will help her when morning dawns. The nations rage, the kingdoms totter; he utters his voice, the earth melts. The LORD of hosts is with us; the God of Jacob is our fortress (Psalm 46:1-7).

The "holy habitation of the Most High" is the people of God, the Body of Christ. Even though great and terrible judgements will come upon the world, and nations will rage against the Lord and His Church, "She shall not be moved," because "God is in the midst of her" and He "is our refuge and strength, a very present help in trouble." We do well to note, however:

1. The true Church consists of those who truly belong to Jesus Christ, who have been born again, regenerated by the Word and the Spirit of God. And those who truly belong to Jesus must not have fellowship with idolatry and unrighteousness. The Lord is using end-time upheavals and trials to sift the vast mixed multitude who profess faith in Christ. Profession

alone is not sufficient to pass the test, and God will not be mocked: "God's firm foundation stands, bearing this seal: 'The Lord knows those who are his,' and, 'Let everyone who names the name of the Lord depart from iniquity'" (2 Tim. 2:19).

2. For the Church in general and believers in particular, victory does not necessarily mean wielding cultural or political influence, or escaping from persecution and pain. In fact, a terrible time is coming when "the beast [will be] permitted to wage war against the saints and to conquer them" (Rev. 13:7). This may appear to be a terrible defeat for the people of God, but it will in fact be a great and celebrated victory, for "they [will] have conquered him [Satan] by the blood of the Lamb and by the word of their testimony, for they loved not their lives even unto death. Therefore, rejoice, O heavens and you who dwell in them!" (Rev. 12:11-12). These saints, though they be killed, will conquer Satan by the blood of Christ, by their faithful testimony, and by being willing to lay down their lives for the Lord. And the host of Heaven will rejoice over their great victory.

Defeat, for Christians, is not being driven from the public square, or losing political battles and legal rights, or being dispossessed, or being persecuted unto death. The only defeat the Church can know is to be unfaithful, for whatever cause, to the Lord and His Word. And from such defeat true believers will be kept, "for the Lord is able to make them stand" (Romans 14:4) and "the one who calls you is faithful and he will do it" (1Thes 5:23).

3. Believers are heading into a worldwide storm of growing intensity. Whether literally or figuratively, the earth will give way, and the

mountains will be moved into the heart of the sea. Our only true shelter is in Christ, who "is our refuge and strength."

The Lord would have us help one another to survive this storm. We can do this through supportive, edifying prayer. God is sovereign, yet He has ordained that we should pray for one another and that our effectual prayers will make a difference. In His excellent wisdom, our praying helps bring one another either deliverance from peril or victory over it. As Paul tells the Corinthians:

We do not want you to be uninformed, brothers and sisters, about the troubles we experienced in the province of Asia. We were under great pressure, far beyond our ability to endure, so that we despaired of life itself. Indeed, we felt we had received the sentence of death. But this happened that we might not rely on ourselves but on God, who raises the dead. He has delivered us from such a deadly peril, and he will deliver us again. On him we have set our hope that he will continue to deliver us, as you help us by your prayers. Then many will give thanks on our behalf for the gracious favour granted us in answer to the prayers of many (2 Cor. 1:8-11).

Whatever happens to us, and whatever the cost, may we trust in the Lord and honour Him: "Now to him who is able to keep you from stumbling and to present you blameless before the presence of his glory with great joy, to the only God, our Saviour, through Jesus Christ our Lord, be glory, majesty, dominion, and authority, before all time and now and forever. Amen" (Jude 24-25).

.

14

3. Learning and Praying God's Will

God knows and cares about our personal needs and desires. He tells us, through the apostle Paul, "don't be anxious about anything, but in everything, by prayer and supplication, with thanksgiving, make your requests known" to Him. But God also has desires and purposes, and His far transcend ours. Yes, He delights to hear His children's requests and to meet our true needs. But He takes even greater delight when we begin to learn from Him, and begin to understand His will, and begin to seek its fulfillment, for His glory. Jesus teaches us to pray, above and before all else, "Hallowed be Thy Name. Thy Kingdom come, Thy will be done." We are to "seek first the Kingdom of God and His righteousness," trusting that as we do this, God will see to all of our true personal necessities.

So, what is God's will, that we may pray that it be done? What does the coming of His Kingdom mean, that we may seek it first? What, we need to know and ought to want to know, does God desire? We need to understand how to pray according to the will of God—which means praying according to His Word—so that we can please the Lord and pray effectually. Thankfully, the Lord is abundantly willing to give us understanding of His will, and I believe the prayer of Jesus recorded in John 17 is the prime source.

4. Jesus Prays the Will of God: John 17

The clearest, most comprehensive and most impassioned statement of God's will is, I believe, the prayer of Jesus recorded in John 17. No other passage in Scripture so fully and profoundly reveals what has moved the heart of God from eternity past and will continue to move it throughout eternity future. This prayer, immediately preceding the Lord's trial and crucifixion, tells us why He is going to the Cross. He is going to the Cross because He desires something that can be obtained only through His own crucifixion and death, something He desires with such intensity that He is willing to make that terrible sacrifice to secure it.

As Jesus faces certain suffering and death at Calvary, one great concern is on His heart and on His mind: the people whom the Father has given Him and will give Him out of the world (v. 6). Nearly the whole of John 17, and the prayer it recounts, consist of the outpouring of the Lord's desire, His will, for His people.

This prayer, the true "Lord's Prayer," lays open before the universe what are inarguably the Son's deepest desires. It is a concise, impassioned summation of the will of God. We do well to understand, by the way, that "God's will" encompasses more than His plans, or that which He wills to perform. It is also the desire propelling His plans. God's will includes His infinitely deep, divine affection for those who put their trust in Him. It is the perfect loving determination of a perfect Father to give His children what is best for them, according to His perfect wisdom, thus making manifest His great glory.

And what is this "best" which God seeks for us and in us? We will begin to examine the particulars in the next chapter. But, in summary, it is the calling out of a people from this world to be His redeemed children,

His Body, His Bride, and to fully live in them, bringing forth in them the perfection of character, love and unity that fit them to glorify Him in this world and to rejoice with Him and with one another for all eternity.

Jesus intends for His people in every generation to hear His prayer in John 17, and to hear it well. He says, as He prays, "These things I speak in the world, that they may have my joy fulfilled in themselves" (v. 12). He lets us overhear His prayer, because our comprehending this, His will—His longing toward us—will fill us with His joy.

It is too easy to gloss over this prayer. Many of us have read it many times, and we know what it's about. But if it hasn't captured our hearts and filled our vision and inspired our own prayers, we haven't read it perceptively or receptively enough!

5. Jesus Prays for the Protection of Believers

The Body of Christ, the Church, is in great need of edification, of wisdom, of growth toward maturity, of more of the knowledge of God, of greater love one member for another, of strength and endurance, of unity. God has promised to supply these necessary blessings to His people as we ask Him for them. His plan is for His Body to come to maturity and to "unity in the faith and in the knowledge of the Son of God" as each part of the Body does the work God has called it to do.

A very important part of our calling, from which none of us is exempt, is to pray for one another, in love, according to the Word. In God's excellent wisdom, each one of us has the capacity to help strengthen and build the Body through effectual prayer. Prayer that seeks for God to be glorified in His Body and for His will to be done in it, that is informed and inspired by the teaching of Scripture, and that is motivated by love, will most certainly please the Lord and be fruitful. It is never in vain that we seek the Lord for His will to be done.

Indeed, the Lord "rewards those who earnestly seek Him" (Heb. 11:6). Concerning our prayer for one another, this reward is twofold: First, requests for edification of the Body, made in love, most definitely will, in some way or another, be granted. Loving, scriptural prayer will be met with answers from the Throne of Grace. And secondly, those who serve the Lord and His people through loving and edifying prayer will receive personal commendation and reward from the Lord—if not now, then certainly in Eternity.

Hear now the apostle Paul commends Epaphras, a "servant of Christ" of whom the Holy Spirit certainly approved: "He is always wrestling in prayer for you, that you may stand firm in all the will of God, mature and fully assured. I vouch for him that he is working hard for you . . . " (Col. 4:12-13). We will examine Epaphras and the wonderful example of his God-pleasing prayer later on.

To pray earnestly for our brothers and sisters in their need (whatever their need) is to love them. It is to be obedient to Christ, who said, "My command is this: Love each other as I have loved you" (John 15:12). There is of course more to loving one another than simply praying for each other, but truly loving prayer will lead to and empower other loving actions. Especially important, prayer helps us to love those believers who, for one reason or another, we feel may not be deserving of our love. Along with the armour of God, loving prayer for all of God's people is an essential part of standing strong in the Lord and in the power of His might (see Eph. 6:18 – 20, of which more later).

Now, getting back to the prayer of Jesus for our protection, recorded in John 17: Jesus prayed, "Holy Father, protect them by the power of your name, the name you gave me, so that they may be one as we are one . . . I have given them your word and the world has hated them, for they are not of the world any more than I am of the world. My prayer is not that you take them out of the world but that you protect them from the evil one. They are not of the world, even as I am not of it" (John 17:10 – 16).

Jesus knew that He was leaving His people, in every generation, to face a hostile world inspired by hateful spirits. His prayer for us was not that we be removed from this world or necessarily protected from its afflictions and persecutions. In the face of external evil, we are "counted as sheep for the slaughter." Rather, Jesus prayed that we would not succumb to evil, that we would be neither seduced nor silenced by it, that we would not be eternally harmed by it. That we would triumph over evil as He did, remaining faithful even unto death.

In our day, spiritual wickedness is rampant and spreading quickly. More and more, the world is hardening itself in direct opposition to the Word of God and those who believe it. For the godly, even in the "enlightened" West, the cost of faithfulness to Christ is steepening. Severe tests of our commitment to the Lord lie ahead. God's people need protection, through the power of the Holy Spirit and the Name of Christ and the truth of the Word, from all concord or compromise with evil.

Let us therefore pray for one another that we may be found faithful, whatever the cost. Let us not rejoice when we see our brothers and sisters falter, but let us pray that they will not fall. Such prayer helps to protect them—and ourselves—from the influence of evil and the condemnation that comes with allowing hostility or unkindness in our hearts.

And let us pray as well for great wisdom for one another, so that we do not entangle the name of Christ with foolish or unprofitable causes and crusades. As Peter wrote: "Keep your conduct among the Gentiles honourable, so that when they speak against you as evildoers, they may see your good deeds and glorify God on the day of visitation" (1 Peter 2:12). If we're going to be persecuted, and we are, may it be for the Name and Word of Christ and not for being mere trouble-makers.

6. Jesus Prays for the Sanctification of Believers

The coronavirus pandemic has placed serious challenges before the people of God. Whether we choose to oppose public health rules or not, they are having a profound effect on believers' lives. And, whether we resist or not, being unable to change the situation to our liking, we must find ways to serve God in it. Thankfully, we know that coronavirus has not taken God by surprise. And we know that He is with us in all circumstances, if we are with Him. Coronavirus cannot prevent God's people from serving Him.

The Lord says something wonderful in the Book of Revelation: "These are the words of the One who is holy and true, who holds the key of David. What He opens no one can shut, and what He shuts no one can open. I know your deeds. See, I have placed before you an open door, which no one can shut" (3:7-8). We don't know the details of the open door Christ had set before the church in Philadelphia in the face of very difficult circumstances. But this passage affirms a principle which applies to all believers in all times, places and situations: God always provides an open door—that is, a way to serve Him and help build in His Kingdom—no matter the circumstances.

We can be confident that God is using the coronavirus "situation" in an endless variety of ways to refine and strengthen His people and to advance His Kingdom. And that, in the face of coronavirus (and other ominous latter-day developments), the Lord is opening innumerable doors which no one can shut.

One great door, which has been open since the Crucifixion, and which remains wide open in every conceivable circumstance, including coronavirus restrictions, is the door to the Father's Throne of Grace in Heaven. Governments may prevent Christians from gathering together, and in time to come they will probably do far worse than this. But they cannot stop us from calling upon God by faith, according to His word, and praying that His Kingdom come and His will be done. Nor can governments stop God from receiving our prayers and answering them in wonderful ways. Men may shut church buildings, but they can never close off that which God has forever set open before us—access through prayer to the Holy of Holies.

It may be that one of the ways the Lord is using coronavirus is to help believers to turn to Him in a fuller way. Now that the world has become less inviting and its pleasures and diversions less accessible, perhaps some of us are finding ourselves drawn or even compelled to seek the Lord as never before. If so, that's a good thing. And if that's the case with you, please give serious thought to these exhortations to make the people of God—the beloved Body and the Bride of Christ—the central focus of your prayers. According to John 17, this is what Jesus did. It is also, as we will see later in numerous passages, what the apostle Paul did. If Jesus did this, and then Paul after Him, we can do no better.

In John 17, after Jesus prays for the protection of those who are His, He prays for our sanctification. We need to understand two key facets of this prayer: what Jesus is asking for, and how it is to be achieved. Sanctification, that blessed process and end-state Jesus desires for us, has a twofold sense. One is a separation from the world, a complete setting apart for and a consecration to God and His purposes. We are in the world, but we are not of the world. We cannot truly live for God while in friendship with the world. We cannot truly live if we are double-minded, trying to perform that impossible straddle between love of this world and love of God. We need to be God's own possession, without reservation. This is what Jesus wants.

The other meaning of sanctification is a purifying, a making holy. True holiness is not obnoxious self-righteousness, but beautiful purity of heart and life, characterized above all by supernatural love. This, also, Jesus wholeheartedly longs to establish in us.

And how is this twofold sanctification to be achieved? Through two great realities. Jesus prays, "Sanctify them by the truth; your word is truth" (v. 17). Only through believing, receiving and applying the Word of God, the truth of the Bible, to our hearts and lives, can God's people be set apart for God and be purified, made holy.

But this is possible only on the basis of Jesus' sacrifice of Himself for us on Calvary: "And for their sake I consecrate myself, that they also may be sanctified in truth" (v. 19). So greatly does Jesus desire our sanctification, which He knows is our best and most blessed state, that He laid down His own life to obtain it for us. Because He who is the Truth has died and risen for us, by His grace we may experience ever-increasing sanctification unto Him.

In conclusion, at least five things are clear:

1. Jesus greatly desires the sanctification of His people. In other words, this is His will. It is what led Him to the Cross. It is what He prayed for in John 17, and it is what He and the Holy Spirit continue to intercede for at this very moment.

2. The Church is in great need of sanctification.

3. Each of us can pray for—and ought to, because it is the clearly revealed will of God—the sanctification of His people. And such prayer is not in vain. Our faithful prayer for the sanctification of the Church will, most certainly, help bring forth the good fruit of sanctification, in due season and in ways which may surprise us.

4. God's answers to our prayers for sanctification will come through the powerful working of the

seed of the truth—His Word—in the good soil of receptive hearts. We therefore need to pray for faithful, fearless and wise preaching and teaching of that Word. Paul's own request for prayer teaches how we might pray for preachers: "Pray also for me, that whenever I speak, words may be given me so that I will fearlessly make known the mystery of the gospel, for which I am an ambassador in chains. Pray that I may declare it fearlessly, as I should" (Eph. 6:19-20).

5. Neither coronavirus nor any other impediment can stop God's work in the earth and in His people. The door is open, and no one can shut it. Let us arise and build. May our effectual, edifying prayer for the people of God help propel the Church forward!

7. Jesus Prays for the Unity of Believers

All who truly belong to Christ are one in Him. Whatever the differences among believers may be, and there are many, we are unified through our relationship to the Lord. As Paul declares, "There is one body and one Spirit—just as you were called to the one hope that belongs to your call—one Lord, one faith, one baptism, one God and Father of all, who is over all and through all and in all (Eph. 4:4-5).

Positionally, God's people are one in Christ. In our manner of living and actual relating to one another, however, we often fall far short of this truth and the high calling to which God has called us. In John 17, Jesus prayed:

> *I do not ask for these only, but also for those who will believe in me through their word, that they may all be one, just as you, Father, are in me, and I in you, that they also may be in us, so that the world may believe that you have sent me. The glory that you have given me I have given to them, that they may be one even as we are one, I in them and you in me, that they may become perfectly one, so that the world may know that you sent me and loved them even as you loved me (20-23).*

God's will is that His people be "perfectly one." That is, unified in the same way that Father, Son and Holy Spirit are. Of course, this would be an utter impossibility if it weren't for the fact that nothing is impossible with God, and that what He has promised, He is able also to perform.

We need to understand two vital things concerning Christian unity: First, that Jesus deeply, passionately desires this and gave His life to make it possible. Our

25

praying "Thy Kingdom come, Thy will be done" ought therefore to echo the Lord's prayer that we become perfectly one. And second, that we cannot just sit around waiting for God to do what He obviously wants to do. Much of what God wills for us, He has determined to accomplish through us. The Lord's desire for the perfect unity of the Church will certainly be fulfilled, but not without our also earnestly desiring it and seeking Him for it.

The perfect unity of the Church depends not upon some momentous, eventual, instantaneous miracle, but upon the growth and development of Christ's character in us, especially love for one another. True unity is a fruit of the necessary and continuing process of wholehearted, loving, mutual edification. God has committed Himself to teaching and equipping us to edify one another in love (Eph. 4). Until we are inclined to learn from Him and obey Him, however, He may just let us wander in the wilderness.

Indeed, it would seem the Church has been wandering in the wilderness of divisiveness and other problems for a long, long time. Far from acknowledging that we are "perfectly one" and that the Father "sent Jesus and loves His people even as He loves Jesus," the world is becoming more sceptical and critical of the Church by the day. This ought not to be. The Lord intends that manifest unity among His people should bear mighty witness to an unbelieving world—and to the spiritual principalities and powers—of His truth and love. Not that the world will necessarily be converted by such witness. But it ought never to find, in weakness and failure and division in the Church, occasion for blasphemy or excuse for rejecting the truth.

In spite of our shortcomings, God has irrevocably identified Himself with us, and us with Himself. Let us therefore seek the honour of His name and the end of all dishonour. As Daniel the prophet prayed, from Babylonian captivity: "O Lord, hear; O Lord, forgive. O Lord, pay attention and act. Delay not, for your own sake, O my God, because your city and your people are called by your name" (Daniel 9:19).

Be encouraged to note, by the way, how God heard and responded to Daniel's fervent prayer, sending an angel to say: "O Daniel, I have now come out to give you insight and understanding. At the beginning of your pleas for mercy a word went out, and I have come to tell it to you, for you are greatly loved. Therefore consider the word and understand the vision" (Daniel 9:22-23). The Lord mightily approved of Daniel's desire to see God's name honoured and His people restored.

There is much to criticize in House of God today, and there is no shortage of critics either outside or inside. Mere criticism, however, is fruitless at best and often destructive. This does not mean that believers must simply ignore problems, weaknesses, sin and failure in the Church. Believers have a responsibility to confront sin and error, to contend for sound doctrine, and to warn of danger. But there are constructive, biblical ways to do these necessary things, and none of them involve mere criticism or finger-pointing.

What the Church needs are sound, biblical responses to problems and needs, motivated always by a commitment to truth and a desire to edify. As Paul says in 1 Cor. 8:1, "love builds up." One great incubator and generator of love in our hearts is effectual prayer— asking God to provide His people with what we need but only He can give, and to do in His people what pleases Him. We may not have the capacity or the responsibility to correct every problem in the Church of which we become aware. But we do have the capacity and responsibility in any situation to pray that God's will be done and that the Church be edified, for His glory. Such prayer will surely help as the "whole structure, being joined together, grows into a holy temple in the Lord. In him you also are being built together into a dwelling place for God by the Spirit" (Eph. 2:21-22).

A word of caution is needed here. The only unity that the Lord desires and commends is unity in Him.

Man-made "unity" of any sort, depending on anything other than the truth of the Word of God and the true knowledge of Jesus Christ, is false and fruitless. May the Lord give us discernment in this matter.

Some may argue that there is no point in praying as Jesus did, that the Church become perfectly one. Some may feel the Church is too messed up and that the Body's condition is hopeless. I cannot agree. Jesus promised to build His Church. He prayed earnestly for our unity, as we have read in John 17, and then went to the Cross in order to secure that for which He prayed. He inspired apostolic teaching on the continuing edification of the Church "until we all attain to the unity of the faith and of the knowledge of the Son of God, to mature manhood, to the measure of the stature of the fullness of Christ" (Eph. 4:13). With eyes of faith on the word of promise, we see God at work "who gives life to the dead and calls into existence the things that do not exist" (Romans 4:17b).

Therefore, "Let us hold fast the confession of our hope without wavering, for he who promised is faithful" (Hebrews 10:23). And let us pray for one another, for local congregations, and for the whole Church, with faith, love and persistence.

8. Jesus Prays that Believers Be With Him and Behold His Glory

In the prayer of Jesus in John 17, we can discern a process or progression of blessing and growth in the lives of God's people. It starts with the Father giving people to the Son out of the world; these are the ones for whom Jesus prays. The Lord asks that each of these be protected and kept safe, in that strong tower which is the Name of the Lord, until their journey through this perilous world is completed. Further, that they be sanctified—made more and more like Christ in consecration, character and purity—through hearing and adhering to the truth of God's Word. Then, that their sanctification and growing up into Christ bring them irresistibly toward unity, just as the spokes of a bicycle wheel converge as they approach the hub. And finally, that believers, having been made ready, ascend to the Saviour, to see and know Him in the unspeakable fullness of His glory: "Father, I want those you have given me to be with me where I am, and to see my glory, the glory you have given me because you loved me before the creation of the world" (John 17:24).

How wonderful it is to contemplate that what our Lord Jesus desires and has planned for His people, what He prayed and still prays for, and what He went to the Cross to accomplish, is to bring us to Himself, into His glorious unveiled presence, there to worship Him and to rejoice with Him and with one another for ever and ever!

Knowing that our eternal blessed union with Jesus is the focus of God's thoughts toward us and of His dealings with us—that this is His ultimate and highest will for each believer—we do well to cultivate within our hearts and prayers something of this same intention for one another. There can be no better prayer for a brother or sister than that they may stand pure and blameless before the Lord when the time comes, and hear Him say, "Well done, good and faithful servant. Enter into the joy of your Lord" (Matthew 25:23). This is God's clearly revealed desire for each of His people, and it pleases Him when we pray for one another according to His will. In due season, we will be thrilled to realize that such prayer, through the gracious working of the Spirit of God, has made a significant difference in the outcome of many lives. And, no less importantly, that it has helped transform and enlarge our own hearts.

Nothing in this life is more important than finishing it well and well-prepared, having run a good race and having fought the good fight. To this end Paul, "the pattern man," devoted himself without reservation to ministering to the people of God: "Him we proclaim, warning everyone and teaching everyone with all wisdom, that we may present everyone mature in Christ. For this I toil, struggling with all His energy that He powerfully works within me" (Col. 1:28-29). "For what is our hope, or joy, or crown of rejoicing? Is it not even you in the presence of our Lord Jesus Christ at His coming? For you are our glory and joy." (1 Thess. 2:19-20). The great reward Paul anticipated for his labours was, very simply, the joy of seeing God's people delighting forever in the presence of the Lord and the glories of Heaven. And, as we will soon see, a major portion of Paul's exceedingly fruitful toil and struggle took place in the arena of prayer.

Maturing in Christ of necessity requires development in ourselves of the very same pure desire toward God's people that filled Jesus and Paul. As we grow in God, we will increasingly seek one another's blessing, particularly eternal blessing. And we will pray with ever-growing love for our brothers and sisters that, whatever their weaknesses or errors or stumbles or offences along the way, they will triumph in the end.

Now please consider this: Making place in our hearts for such love and prayer actually helps us prepare ourselves, as well as those for whom we pray, for the great Day that is approaching. To quote another wonderful prayer of Paul: "May the Lord make you increase and abound in love for one another and for all, as we do for you, so that He may establish your hearts blameless in holiness before our God and Father, at the coming of our Lord Jesus with all His saints" (1 Thess. 12-13). At the coming of the Lord, He will want to see us abounding in love for one another.

God is calling His people into the much-needed work of prayer that, according to His will and Word, builds up the Body of Christ. Although we may be weak, we can trust that, if we are willing, then through His grace we can be effectual and fruitful in this labour.

9. The Prayer of Jesus in the Prayers of Paul

The apostle Paul had both deep insight into the purposes of God for the Church, and deep love for the people of God. He wrote, in all sincerity and truth: "God can testify how I long for all of you with the affection of Christ Jesus" (Phil 1:8). Paul's prayer life was a relentless pursuit of that will revealed by Jesus in John 17, in the same self-giving love demonstrated by Jesus at the Cross.

Paul's numerous afflictions, sufferings, beatings and imprisonments amply prove his all-consuming commitment to the Gospel and to the people of God. And so do his prayers. Paul's prayers reveal, as we will see, a heart filled with Christ's love for the Church, burning with a vision of the glory to which the Lord has called His people. Paul earnestly desired, just as Jesus does, for each of us to fulfill God's will and to stand before Him, joyful and fully assured, at the end of this present life. His prayers sought the will of Christ by the power and inspiration of the Spirit of Christ.

And Paul's prayers were very, very effectual. They helped bring the full power and conviction of the Holy Spirit upon his teaching, missionary work and defence of the Gospel. And they greatly influenced and edified the people for whom he prayed, including the Christians of every generation, including ours. Paul, a mighty builder in the House of God, sought and found power, wisdom and grace to build on his knees, at the Throne of Grace.

What does all of this mean for believers today, particularly with regard to prayer? It means that God has graciously given us, through Paul's epistles, marvellous instruction, guidance and inspiration for effectually seeking Him. We would be foolish to leave such gifts unopened and unused. Seeking God while remaining ignorant or dismissive of Paul's example and instruction would be like entering a wrestling match with your better hand tied behind your back. And your legs tied together.

10. Following Paul's Example in Prayer

The Lord gave to Paul a superabundance of grace, revelation, insight and authority. His purpose in doing this was not to exalt a mere man, but to build up and extend His Church, and to establish the truths and principles by which the Church should conduct itself until the return of Christ. Clearly, God made Paul a "pattern man," one who could say with all sincerity and authority, "Follow my example, as I follow the example of Christ," and "Whatever you have learned or received or heard from me, or seen in me—put it into practice. And the God of peace will be with you."

Scripture testifies that Paul's teaching was foundational, and his manner of life and ministry exemplary, to a degree surpassing even that of the other apostles. Consider these passages, written by Paul under the inspiration of the Holy Spirit:

> *Even though you have ten thousand guardians in Christ, you do not have many fathers, for in Christ Jesus I became your father through the gospel. Therefore I urge you to imitate me. For this reason I am sending to you Timothy, my son, whom I love, who is faithful in the Lord. He will remind you of my way of life in Christ Jesus, which agrees with what I teach everywhere in every church* (1 Cor. 4:15-17).

> *Follow my example, as I follow the example of Christ. I praise you for remembering me in everything and for holding to the teachings, just as I passed them on to you* (1 Cor. 11:1-2).

> *Join with others in following my example, brothers, and take note of those who live according to the pattern we gave you* (Phil. 3:17).

Whatever you have learned or received or heard from me, or seen in me—put it into practice. And the God of peace will be with you (Phil. 4:9).

But for that very reason I was shown mercy so that in me, the worst of sinners, Christ Jesus might display his unlimited patience as an example for those who would believe on him and receive eternal life (1 Tim. 1:16).

What you have heard from me, keep as the pattern of sound teaching, with faith and love in Christ Jesus. Guard the good deposit that was entrusted to you—guard it with the help of the Holy Spirit who lives in us (2 Tim. 1:13).

God assigned to Paul his ministry as the Church's foundation-layer and prime exemplar of the God-pleasing Christian life. When Paul says, "Follow my example, as I follow the example of Christ," we can receive it as though the Lord were saying, "Paul is a man who has my full approval. I have made him who he is and worked in him the way I have, for your benefit. Follow his teaching and his manner of life, and I will be with you."

I believe that we are called to follow Paul's example in prayer, of which we have ample documentation in his letters. As we learn the specifics of what Paul prayed for, and perceive the heart with which he prayed, and as in simple faith and obedience we seek to follow his example, our prayer lives will be transformed. Our attitude toward other believers will change. Our hearts will be enlarged with Christ's love and filled with a vision of God's glorious plan for His people. Our faith, feeding on the truth of the Word, will grow. Our prayers, truly seeking the declared will of God, will greatly please the Father and become more and more effectual. And, having sought the good of God's people in prayer, we may well find ourselves being used by God outside the prayer closet to bring strength and healing to the Body, with a fit word in due season or other ministration of His grace and truth.

11. Paul Prays for the Sanctification of Believers

We know that when Paul prayed for the saints, he prayed by the inspiration of the Holy Spirit, according to the desires of Jesus for His Church. For this reason, Paul's prayers are worthy of our receptive study. They clearly illuminate the will of God—that is, those things for which we ought to pray. And they model, just as clearly, the steadfastness and affection with which we ought to pray for one another.

For this same reason, Paul's prayers are also well worth adopting as our own. The apostle's exhortation to Timothy, "What you have heard from me, keep as the pattern of sound teaching, with faith and love in Christ Jesus" (2 Tim 1:13), applies as much to his praying as to anything else he taught or modeled. The Church has no better example of the edifying, God-pleasing, effectual Christian prayer life than what we see in Paul. The prayers of Paul constitute a large part of the biblical standard by which we must evaluate all teaching and practice of prayer that we encounter. Any doctrine or practice of prayer which disregards or contradicts this clear guidance of Scripture will at the very least miss out on the fullness of God's wisdom and blessings.

So it is with Paul's prayers for the sanctification of God's people. Just as the Lord Jesus did, as recorded in John 17, Paul earnestly sought after the purification of believers and their full consecration to God. For, "without holiness, no one shall see the Lord" (Hebrews 12:14). Can the same be said about contemporary prayer? Does sanctification, so highly valued by the Lord and so greatly needed by His people, receive even mention, much less due emphasis, in various current teachings about prayer? Does it ever appear on church prayer request lists? Or has it been crowded out by spurious notions and pleas for temporal—and temporary—blessings?

Paul's overarching desire for all believers was that at the end of this one, short, unrepeatable earthly journey toward eternity, we would stand pure, blameless, and ready to meet the Lord: "He is the one we proclaim, admonishing and teaching everyone with all wisdom, so that we may present everyone fully mature in Christ. To this end I strenuously contend with all the energy Christ so powerfully works in me" (Col. 1:28-29). "Fully mature," also translated "perfect," means sanctified, purified and conformed to Christ in every way. Sanctification, above all else, is what each of us will need in order to stand joyfully "on that Day." Should we not therefore make it a matter of earnest, persistent prayer now?

Presenting believers mature and blameless before the Lord was not only the central purpose of Paul's ministry, it was also the great reward he anticipated in eternity: "For what is our hope, our joy, or the crown in which we will glory in the presence of our Lord Jesus when he comes? Is it not you?" (1 Thess. 2:19). To see God's people rejoicing before the Lord, having overcome the world, the flesh and the devil, was Paul's fondest hope and greatest joy. And thus he prayed:

"May God himself, the God of peace, sanctify you through and through. May your whole spirit, soul and body be kept blameless at the coming of our Lord Jesus Christ. The one who calls you is faithful and he will do it" (1Thess. 5:23-24). As with all of Paul's prayers, we can—and ought to—pray in the same way. And we should note in this prayer that, although God Himself does the sanctifying, and He is faithful in accomplishing it, He has ordained that our prayer for one another should be a vital help in the process. To the extent we seek and aid the sanctification of God's people, we will share Paul's joy at seeing our brothers and sisters delighting in the presence of the Lord "on that Day."

Here is another of Paul's prayers for sanctification. He is praying for the Corinthians, who had been tolerating grievous sin in their midst and who needed to put this sin away and cleanse themselves: "Now we pray to God that you will not do anything wrong. Not that people will see that we have stood the test but that you will do what is right even though we may seem to have failed" (2 Cor. 13:7). This straightforward prayer seeks simply that the Corinthians will receive the necessary grace and conviction from God to do what is right. Paul prayed in this way because he knew this sanctification was the will of God and that his prayer would help.

With typical selflessness, Paul assures the Corinthians that he isn't concerned about how their response to his correction may affect his reputation. He doesn't want them to comply so that he will be seen as an effective, successful minister. He simply wants them to do what is right for their own sake, even if it makes him look bad. He then goes on to write, "We are glad whenever we are weak but you are strong; and our prayer is for your perfection [restoration, sanctification]" (2 Cor. 13:9).

12. Paul Prays for Believers to Know God Better

In Paul's epistles, there are at least 30 passages (see Appendix) in which the apostle prays, exhorts believers to pray, or requests prayer. These instructive, inspiring verses echo and amplify the prayer of Jesus in John 17. That is, what Jesus desired and asked the Father for in John 17, Paul continues to desire and ask the Father for: the protection, sanctification, unification and bringing to glory of the people of God. This makes perfect sense. Paul, filled with the Spirit of Christ, seeks the very things from the Father that Jesus did. And we, if we have that same Spirit, will do so as well.

Paul's prayers add detail and definition to the very concise prayer of Jesus in John 17. They reveal the wonderful range of rich blessings we have been given the liberty and confidence to seek for one another at the Throne of Grace. What's more, as a perceptive British preacher, Alexander McLaren, realized many years ago, "Paul's prayers are God's promises." What this means is that, whatever Paul prayed for, the Lord must have wanted (and still wants) to give. The Holy Spirit would never inspire Paul to pray for anything for believers which was not in full accord with the desire and purposes of God.

We can therefore be confident that the wonderful blessings sought by Paul for the Church are exactly what God desires to bestow upon us today. But the Lord does require that we ask for them. This isn't because He needs our help. God has ordained for us to pray so that He may work great, essential, eternal good in us as we do. So, let's consider Paul's first prayer for the Ephesians (1:16-23):

For this reason, ever since I heard about your faith in the Lord Jesus and your love for all God's people, I have not stopped giving thanks for you, remembering you in my prayers. I keep asking that the God of our Lord Jesus Christ, the glorious Father, may give you the Spirit of wisdom and revelation, so that you may know him better. I pray that the eyes of your heart may be enlightened in order that you may know the hope to which he has called you, the riches of his glorious inheritance in his holy people, and his incomparably great power for us who believe. That power is the same as the mighty strength he exerted when he raised Christ from the dead and seated him at his right hand in the heavenly realms, far above all rule and authority, power and dominion, and every name that is invoked, not only in the present age but also in the one to come. And God placed all things under his feet and appointed him to be head over everything for the church, which is his body, the fullness of him who fills everything in every way.

In this prayer we can perceive the pattern which characterized Paul's praying. We would do very well to follow his example in these things:

1. Paul prayed.

In this instance, for the Christians in Ephesus. As we will discover in his other epistles, it seems he prayed for all the believers and every church of which he had knowledge or with which he had contact. What does this mean for us? It means that prayer is essential. Even the great apostle Paul could not carry out his mission without it. If prayer were unnecessary and fruitless, Paul would not have prayed. God is gracious and generous beyond our comprehension but, according to His excellent wisdom, He would have us in a constant state of confident dependency upon Him. We must ask, and when we ask, we receive.

2. Paul prayed for others, with love.

Paul's heart was filled with love and affection for the people of God, and he sought their blessing and edification in prayer. In doing so, he obeyed the command of Jesus, that we love one another.

3. Paul prayed in genuine faith, expecting answers.

He earnestly sought the living God for real, glorious things that only the Lord could give, believing that He answers such prayers.

4. Paul prayed with the confidence of a child before a loving Father.

Paul knew that, through the blood of Christ, he had full access to the Throne of Grace.

5. Paul prayed persistently.

"I keep asking," he writes. He knew that the Church had continuing, unending need for that which only the Spirit of God can supply. He knew also that, whatever believers may have received already, God had much more to bestow on them out of his vast store of riches in glory. In season or out of season, Paul never stopped asking.

6. Paul prayed for wonderful, much-needed spiritual blessings.

Throughout his epistles, he relates what he is asking for: the blessing, edification and empowerment of the saints so that they will please the Lord, being filled with the Spirit and His fruit, maturing in Christ, growing in wisdom and unity, and preparing for "that Day." Paul was building for eternity. His life and prayer life were focussed on preparing God's people for their glorious heavenly destiny.

7. Paul prayed with thanksgiving.

8. Paul prayed so that God would be glorified.

Paul asks, in this passage, for the Spirit of wisdom and revelation. He is asking God to give the Holy Spirit to His people so that we can know God more fully, and understand things that we need to understand but don't yet understand. Glorious things—like the knowledge of God Himself—that can be truly known only by revelation from God. Note that the Ephesians had already been filled with the Holy Spirit (Eph. 1:13-14). Yet they needed continue to receive more of the Holy Spirit, and to know God better.

I would urge you to read and reread this prayer, with utmost receptivity. What Paul is asking for here, the Church desperately needs and the Lord generously wants to give. Through the shedding of His own blood, The Lord has made a way for us to approach the Throne of Grace and, with confidence, to seek Him for these very things.

We have the wonderful privilege of praying in this way. We can pray for the believers that we know, for the people in our churches, for the churches in our communities, and for Christians around the world. We can freely ask God to give us the Spirit of wisdom and revelation. We need the Holy Spirit. We can't truly live without the Holy Spirit. We need to know God better. We need to know—to have our eyes opened to see—what a great hope He is calling us to, and how greatly it excels the things of this present world.

We need to know and desire the glorious inheritance we have in Christ. We need to know the mighty power God is most willing and able to exercise in us who believe. He wants us to know that His power at work in us is the very power that raised Christ from the dead. Whatever our present state may be, His power is able to restore, sanctify and transform us so that we grow up into Christ and bear much fruit for the glory of God.

Lord, we are willing but we are weak. Help us to ask, in faith and love, persistently, according to your

Word-revealed will, that we and all of your people may receive what you overwhelmingly desire to give!

13. Paul Prays for Love to Abound in Believers

The apostle Paul was an extremely tough man. He endured a life of almost unimaginable physical hardship: "I have worked much harder, been in prison more frequently, been flogged more severely, and been exposed to death again and again. Five times I received from the Jews the forty lashes minus one. Three times I was beaten with rods, once I was pelted with stones, three times I was shipwrecked, I spent a night and a day in the open sea, I have been constantly on the move. I have been in danger from rivers, in danger from bandits, in danger from my fellow Jews, in danger from Gentiles; in danger in the city, in danger in the country, in danger at sea; and in danger from false believers. I have laboured and toiled and have often gone without sleep; I have known hunger and thirst and have often gone without food; I have been cold and naked" (2 Cor. 11:23-27).

Paul also faced the emotional and mental stress of murderous opposition and harsh criticism, as well as abandonment and betrayal by disloyal believers. Unlike some other apostles, he had none of the comforts or support of a home, a wife and children.

One might expect a man who had suffered so much to be calloused or even bitter. But Paul, in spite of all of the opposition and adversity he experienced, remained content, thankful and even joyful in the Lord. And his heart continually overflowed with tender love for the people of God: " . . . We were gentle among you, like a nursing mother taking care of her own children. So, being affectionately desirous of you, we were ready to share with you not only the gospel of God but also our own selves, because you had become very dear to us" (1 Thess. 2:7-8).

What amazing grace Paul had received from the Lord! Even when it was necessary for him to exercise apostolic authority in defence of the Gospel and the purity of the Church, he did so with gentleness and longsuffering. He gave the Corinthians, who had been tolerating grievous sin in their midst, time and opportunity to avoid what would be, for them, a painful in-person confrontation: "For this reason I write these things while I am away from you, that when I come I may not have to be severe in my use of the authority that the Lord has given me for building up and not for tearing down" (2 Cor. 13:10).

Paul recognized that his calling was to edify the Church in love. The Lord had put supernatural love in his heart for the people of God, and seeking their best motivated everything he said and did, and all of his prayers. As he wrote to the Philippians, "God can testify how I long for all of you with the affection of Christ Jesus" (Phil. 1:8). This declaration of affection was not an idle platitude. Paul called God as witness to his God-given love for the Philippians (which same love, no doubt, he also had for all the saints everywhere).

Note also that Paul's love was more than a mere strong emotion of affection. He "longed for" the Philippians. What did this mean? Paul's love for them, which was Christ's love working in him, sought good for them. Paul's all-consuming purpose was that they be fully conformed to Christ, standing firm and fully assured in Him, coming to maturity in Him. He desired that they be strong in the Lord and in the power of His might, filled with the knowledge of God and the fruit of the Spirit, impervious to the lure of the world and the assaults of the enemy. We see Paul's similar longing desire toward the Galatians, "my little children, for whom I am again in the anguish of childbirth until Christ is formed in you!" (Gal. 4:19).

Paul then told the Philippians that he was praying that this same supernatural love that God put in his heart for them would fill their hearts as well: "And this is my prayer: that your love may abound more and more in knowledge and depth of insight, so that you may be able to discern what is best and may be pure and blameless until the day of Christ, filled with the fruit of righteousness that comes through Jesus Christ—to the glory and praise of God" (Phil. 1:9-11).

Please note, in connection with this marvellous prayer:

1. It is the will of God that His people abound in love—for the Lord, for His word, for one another, and for those outside the faith.

2. Paul prayed that the Philippians' love "may abound more and more" because he knew, through the inspiration of the Holy Spirit, that this was the will of God, and that praying in this way is effectual in helping to advance the purposes of God. He knew that praying in this way is to pray, "Thy Kingdom come, Thy will be done."

3. Twenty centuries later, believers also can, and ought to, pray in the very same way. As Paul wrote further along in the same epistle to the Philippians: "What you have learned and received and heard and seen in me—practice these things, and the God of peace will be with you" (Phil. 4:9). Do believers today need to abound in love? Of course we do. Is the Lord pleased when we pray like this? Of course He is. Will He answer such prayer? Of course He will.

4. As we pray in this way for others, we can pray also for ourselves, that our own love will abound more and more. Jesus commands us to love one another, but this does not come naturally. We need the grace of God and the power of the Holy Spirit to love others in a way that pleases the Lord. When we ask Him to fill us with this grace and love, He will be faithful to enlarge our hearts.

5. It is not possible to truly discern the will of God, nor what is best in the sight of God, nor how properly to apply the Word of God, without love. Love is essential to godly understanding, and without it there can be no standing "pure and blameless" before God.

6. In contrast to this present world's highly destructive misconception of love, God's love is not "sloppy agape" or indiscriminate tolerance. God's love is inseparable from His truth. His love is wise, knowing, discerning and pure. Godly love loves truth and righteousness: "Love takes no pleasure in evil, but rejoices in the truth" (1 Cor. 13:6).

7. God's truth produces love in those who receive it, as this prayer passage in Philippians powerfully demonstrates. Paul writes to Timothy: "The purpose of my instruction is that all believers would be filled with love that comes from a pure heart, a clear conscience, and genuine faith" (1 Tim. 1:5). The claim that true obedience to Scripture produces hate, bigotry or any such wickedness, is simply false. As is the notion that impure, defiled, unbelieving hearts are capable of true love.

Father, please fill our hearts with pure love—for You, for your Word, for your people, and for those who do not know You. Our own feeble, fickle "love" will never do. We, your people, need to be filled with the mighty "affection of Jesus Christ," which comes from You alone. You are abundantly willing and able to cause your wise, discerning love to abound in us, so please do it, Lord. Give us the grace to seek this love faithfully and persistently, for the edification of your Church and the glory of your Name!

14. Paul Prays for Believers to Know the Will of God

In every one of his epistles, the apostle Paul prays for, or relates how he is praying for, those to whom he is writing. These prayers, inspired by the Holy Spirit, reveal much:

1. They reveal the chief priorities of God's will for His people. Whatever Paul prays for, God wants to do and desires to give. Summed up, these prayers reveal God's will for His people to come to maturity, unity and fullness in Christ.

2. They reveal Paul's Holy Spirit-inspired heart of steadfast affection toward God's people.

3. They reveal Paul's constant, persistent commitment to the edification of the people of God.

4. They reveal for what and for whom God would have believers in every generation pray.

5. They reveal the motivation and attitude with which God would have us pray.

Believers praying consistently and persistently according to the example Paul has given us will bring great blessing upon the Church. By the grace of God, I desire and intend to do this very thing for the rest of my life.

The answers to such wonderful prayers amount to nothing less than what many would call "revival," or a glorious awakening to God among His people. I believe such awakening will come as and when God's people seek Him for it through scriptural prayer. But such biblical awakening will be marked by holiness, love, joy, wisdom, maturity, unity and other good fruits and gifts of the Spirit rather than by fanatical excesses, dubious manifestations and questionable "wonders," none of which are sought by Jesus in John 17, nor by Paul in his prayers.

Consider Paul's powerful prayer for the Colossians, 1:9-12. Note, particularly, the effects of being truly filled with the knowledge of God's will, following "in order that":

> *For this reason, since the day we heard about you, we have not stopped praying for you and asking God to fill you with the knowledge of his will through all spiritual wisdom and understanding. And we pray this in order that you may live a life worthy of the Lord and may please him in every way: bearing fruit in every good work, growing in the knowledge of God, being strengthened with all power according to his glorious might so that you may have great endurance and patience, and joyfully giving thanks to the Father, who has qualified you to share in the inheritance of the saints in the kingdom of light* (Colossians 1:9-12).

These fruits or blessings are what God wills in the lives of those who love Him; or, in other words, they are the result of our understanding and desiring to do God's will:

1. We seek to live lives worthy of the Lord

2. We seek to please the Lord in every way

3. We bear fruit in every good work

4. We grow in the knowledge of God

5. We are greatly strengthened to face trials and suffering with endurance and patience

6. We joyfully give thanks to the Father, knowing that He has given us a glorious inheritance through Christ

Just as Paul did for the Colossians, we can pray for one another that God will fill us with the knowledge of His will in all spiritual wisdom and understanding. God's will isn't primarily a matter of external "direction"—which school to attend, what career to follow, whether or not to be a missionary, etc.

Rather, it is a matter of inward conformity to the character of Christ, seeking Him according to His Word, and bearing fruit daily for His glory. If we have our hearts set on these things, we can absolutely trust the Lord to lead and guide us in the lesser, external matters that tend to dominate and mystify our conception of "God's will."

15. Paul Prays for the Encouragement of Believers

For Christians, life can be desperately difficult and painful at times—even in a comparatively prosperous, civil and peaceful society. In spite of our hopes, prayers and best efforts, things can go very wrong. Physical afflictions, financial troubles and interpersonal issues can threaten to overwhelm us. And sometimes our own sin and failures can lead us to despair of ever rejoicing in victory.

The psalmist wrote, in deep discouragement, "My soul is cast down within me" as he remembered better days (Psalm 42:6). His experience is typical of believers in the process of becoming "steadfast, immovable, always abounding in the work of the Lord" (1 Cor. 15:58). Shaking must happen in our lives. It alone can teach us to grasp, with all of our hearts, that which cannot be shaken. Thankfully, even in our lowest moments, when our circumstances and feelings may suggest that God has forgotten us, His faithful testimony stands: "Surely I am with you always, to the very end of the age" (Matt. 28:20).

The apostle Paul endured many personal afflictions, trials and discouragements. His life exemplified the paradox of Christian suffering, which is that our pains and afflictions, through a miracle of God's grace, prepare and and incline our hearts to minister true life to others. Paul wrote to the Corinthians, "For we who live are always being given over to death for Jesus' sake, so that the life of Jesus also may be manifested in our mortal flesh. So death is at work in us, but life in you" (2 Cor. 4:7 8). The loss and suffering the Lord ordained or permitted in Paul's life enabled him the more fully to bless others and to lead them into fuller life in Christ. For Paul, this was a most worthwhile exchange.

The consistently edifying and encouraging nature of Paul's prayers is striking, especially when compared with some of the "prayers" offered in homes and churches today. Many believers—and their children—will have encountered preachy or scolding "prayers," by which the person praying isn't so much asking the Lord for help as delivering a sermon or a reproof to someone. Many of us have likely been guilty of "praying" in this way ourselves. I know I have. Such patently unbiblical prayers simply fall flat and deflate the hearers. But Paul shows us a better way to pray—earnestly, and with love, seeking genuine spiritual blessing and victory for God's people. And his prayers, while not at all "preachy," embody tremendous truth.

Here's a wonderful example, from Paul's letter to the Colossians: "I want you to know how much I am struggling for you and for those at Laodicea, and for all who have not met me personally. My purpose is that they may be encouraged in heart and united in love, so that they may have the full riches of complete understanding, in order that they may know the mystery of God, namely, Christ, in whom are hidden all the treasures of wisdom and knowledge" (Col 2:1-3).

Being distant from the Colossian believers, and knowing their true needs, he struggled for them in prayer. And not only for them, but also for believers he hadn't even met. Such is the unlimited scope of the edifying prayer life to which God graciously calls us. Paul's wholehearted desire for the saints, engaging his whole being in prayer for them, is to encourage them so that they might comprehend and possess the true riches and treasures that are the knowledge of Christ.

This is the will of God for His people! This pattern of prayer is not in the Bible by accident, or to fill up pages with empty verbiage. It conveys the will of God, as to both the attitude with which we should pray, and those things for which we should pray. Such an example of edifying and encouraging and Christ-seeking prayer, directly inspired by the Holy Spirit, we do very well to follow!

Here is another of Paul's prayers for encouragement, brief but packed with grace and substance: "May our Lord Jesus Christ himself and God our Father, who loved us and by his grace gave us eternal encouragement and good hope, encourage your hearts and strengthen you in every good deed and word" (II Thess 2:16-17).

Note that it is the Lord Himself (Himself!) who encourages us. The Creator of the universe has already said to us, "Let not your hearts be troubled, neither let them be afraid" (John 14:27). And He is ready to draw near and remind us of His unfailing love, especially as we seek Him for one another. Note also that God's encouragement brings not merely a brighter outlook, but the strength to serve Him and to testify of His goodness.

As we pray for one another according to the wonderful guidance of Scripture, several things will happen. Our faith will grow, as we realize more and more that such prayer is according to God's will and that it pleases Him. Our love for others will grow, supernaturally, because that's what happens when we seek God's best for others. And we ourselves will be encouraged as we please God and love others. And, in due season, we will see answers from the Throne of Grace. May the Lord, therefore, encourage our hearts and strengthen us in every good deed and word—and prayer!

16. Paul Prays for the Unity of Believers

We know that God's will is for His people to come to unity in Christ, and it seems clear that He wills for it to happen in this present world, before His return. Jesus prayed, "I do not ask for these only, but also for those who will believe in me through their word, that they may all be one, just as you, Father, are in me, and I in you, that they also may be in us, so that the world may believe that you have sent me. The glory that you have given me I have given to them, that they may be one even as we are one, I in them and you in me, that they may become perfectly one, so that the world may know that you sent me and loved them even as you loved me" (John 17:20-23).

We know that the eventual unity of believers in Christ is certain, the result of a process of edification and growth over time: "And he gave the apostles, the prophets, the evangelists, the shepherds and teachers, to equip the saints for the work of ministry, for building up the body of Christ, until we all attain to the unity of the faith and of the knowledge of the Son of God, to mature manhood, to the measure of the stature of the fullness of Christ" (Eph. 4:11-13).

We know, from the passage just quoted, that true Christian unity springs from two things: a common faith, or comprehension of and commitment to God's one saving doctrine as revealed in Scripture; and, equally, from a common knowledge of Jesus Christ. Is there a difference between comprehension of the faith and knowledge of the Son of God? Evidently so, because Paul makes the distinction. Proper reception of "the faith" leads to the knowledge of the Son of God. It is not possible to know God without hearing and believing the truth He has revealed about Himself through Scripture. But actually knowing God is not the same as knowing Scripture.

Actually knowing God is essential both to true Christian unity and to joyful entrance into the Lord's eternal Kingdom: "And this is eternal life, that they know you, the only true God, and Jesus Christ whom you have sent" (John 17:3). "On that day" the Lord will say to some who will claim to have served Him, "I never knew you. Away from me, you evildoers!" (Matt. 7:23).

Concerning unity, we might as well be honest: If it weren't for the fact that Jesus wills for His people to become perfectly one, and that He is able to perform what He has promised, it would be an utterly lost cause. Humanly speaking, the Church today is woefully fractured and divided. Not only are Christians mired in disunity and visible disagreement on countless fronts, it seems few are even much concerned about this fact and the way it dishonours the Lord. Absent a mighty, deep, gracious work of God, the Bride of Christ will be anything but presentable when the Lord presents her to Himself.

Some will argue that the Body of Christ is indeed one, that there is no division in Christ, that those who truly belong to Him are truly one in Him. This reasoning is true, but only partly so, and it misses the point. Jesus prayed that His people would be "perfectly one," so manifestly united, that the world would have to acknowledge that Jesus has come from God and lives among His people. Does the Church consistently, clearly bear such a witness to the world today? No, it certainly doesn't.

Thankfully, we serve the One who "gives life to the dead and calls into existence the things that do not exist" (Rom. 4:17b). We need to emulate Abraham's faith in the face of admittedly discouraging facts: "No unbelief made him waver concerning the promise of God, but he grew strong in his faith as he gave glory to

God, fully convinced that God was able to do what he had promised" (Rom. 4:20-21).

As quoted above, Jesus prayed for the unity of God's people. So did Paul: "May the God who gives endurance and encouragement give you a spirit of unity among yourselves as you follow Christ Jesus, so that with one heart and mouth you may glorify the God and Father of our Lord Jesus Christ" (Rom 15:5-6).

Note that true unity comes from God, and only from God. It comes through His mighty working as we "follow Jesus Christ"—both by keeping His Word ("the faith") and seeking His face (i.e., "the knowledge of the Son of God"). And note that, ultimately, true unity is seen when all of God's people give glory to God as if we were one man with one heart and one mouth. Paul prays for this spirit of unity, not because it had already filled the people of God, but because it hadn't. So we also can and ought to pray, persistently, in the same way.

In his letter to the Colossians, Paul relates how earnestly he is seeking unity among the believers: "I want you to know how much I am struggling for you and for those at Laodicea, and for all who have not met me personally. My purpose is that they may be encouraged in heart and united in love, so that they may have the full riches of complete understanding, in order that they may know the mystery of God, namely, Christ, in whom are hidden all the treasures of wisdom and knowledge" (Col. 2:1-3).

Note the edifying, virtuous cycle these verses suggest: Being united in love leads to, or is conducive to, finding the knowledge of God. And, as we have already seen, the vice versa applies: The knowledge of God among believers produces unity.

The Lord's clearly revealed will is to display His manifold wisdom, through a mature, sanctified, unified Church, to the unbelieving world and to its ruling principalities and powers (John 17:23; Eph. 3:10). Yet many believers today seem instead to obsessively be pursuing signs, wonders, healings and miracles. Such infatuation with the miraculous would suggest that God has no greater interest or desire than to put His power over matter on display for the Church and the world.

But this approach is getting things backward. According to the prayer of Jesus for His Body in John 17, and Paul's many inspired, apostolic prayers for believers, God's priority is that His people be edified and sanctified, that we be conformed to Christ, and that we come to maturity, unity and fullness in Him. The Lord seeks fruit that will last, and this is brought forth through the long, slow, patient process of growing up into Christ, according to His Word. There is no miraculous short-cut to spiritual edification and growth.

It is certain, however, that, as we give due attention to that which God has clearly told us He desires, and as we pray "Thy Kingdom come, Thy will be done" according to His heart and Word, and as we are conformed to Christ, and as His glorious name is highly honoured through the wise and sanctified conduct of His people, He will be greatly pleased.

Then, surely, He will bestow glorious tokens of His pleasure, as in the earliest church, when "those who believed were of one heart and soul" and "great grace was upon them all" (Acts 4:32-33). In fact, as Psalm 33 says, He will command the blessing. And what a blessing it is:

> Behold, how good and pleasant it is when brothers dwell in unity! It is like the precious oil on the head, running down on the beard, on the beard of Aaron, running down on the collar of his robes! It is like the dew of Hermon, which falls on the mountains of Zion! For there the LORD has commanded the blessing, life forevermore.

I must add a vital caveat: There is one true unity in Christ, unity in "the" faith and in "the" knowledge of the Son of God. This unity is possible only through the work of the Almighty in His people. Outside of the working of God, there are also various man-made religious "unity" movements in the world. Ecumenical and interfaith attempts to achieve "unity" all entail denial or compromise of "the faith," the biblical revelation, that was once for all delivered to the saints. They lack "the knowledge of the Son of God." All such movements are to be discerned and avoided.

17. Paul Prays for Wisdom and Understanding for Believers

How God's people require wisdom in this hour. Thankfully, the Lord is abundantly willing to give it to us. We need only draw near to Him in faith and receive: "If any of you lacks wisdom, let him ask God, who gives generously to all without reproach, and it will be given him" (James 1:5). The Holy Spirit imparts wisdom by illuminating the written Word within hungry and attentive hearts. The greatest of wisdom's glorious treasures is the knowledge of the Lord Himself:

My child, if you receive my words and treasure up my commandments with you, making your ear attentive to wisdom and inclining your heart to understanding; yes, if you call out for insight and raise your voice for understanding, if you seek it like silver and search for it as for hidden treasures, then you will understand the fear of the LORD and find the knowledge of God. For the LORD gives wisdom; from his mouth come knowledge and understanding (Proverbs 2:1-6).

May the Lord make our ears attentive to wisdom and incline our hearts to understanding. And may we also pray for wisdom and understanding for one another, as the apostle Paul demonstrates:

I have not stopped giving thanks for you, remembering you in my prayers. I keep asking that the God of our Lord Jesus Christ, the glorious Father, may give you the Spirit of wisdom and revelation, so that you may know him better (Eph. 1:16-17).

Since the day we heard about you, we have not stopped praying for you and asking God to fill you with the knowledge of his will through all spiritual wisdom and understanding (Col. 1:9).

I want you to know how much I am struggling for you and for those at Laodicea, and for all who have not met me personally. My purpose is that they may be encouraged in heart and united in love, so that they may have the full riches of complete understanding, in order that they may know the mystery of God, namely, Christ, in whom are hidden all the treasures of wisdom and knowledge (Col. 2:1-3).

There is much to glean from these passages, but here are three brief observations:

1. Paul made this kind of edifying prayer for the saints a persistent, lifelong practice: "I have not stopped . . . I keep asking . . . we have not stopped . . ." Such determined persistence is essential to receiving abundantly from God. There's no way around it.

2. The ultimate definition and end of wisdom is the knowledge of God. Nothing is more to be desired than knowing God, whom to know is true life: "And this is eternal life, that they know you, the only true God, and Jesus Christ whom you have sent" (John 17:3).

3. The Lord graciously desires, far more than we can comprehend, that we know Him in fullness. He has "blessed us with every spiritual blessing in the heavenly realms" (Eph. 1:3) and longs for us to possess these blessings. So when we set our hearts to receive from Him, He will surely give : "I am the LORD your God . . . Open your mouth wide, and I will fill it" (Psalm 81:10)

This present world is losing all restraint, descending into a roiling, reeling vortex of restless evil and aggrievement. Even believers are at risk of being swept into the firestorm of indignation, fury and harsh, untamed rhetoric. But whatever wrongs and injustices we may suffer, we need to remain "wise in the way we act toward outsiders, making the most of every opportunity." May our words always be gracious, seasoned with salt, so that we may know how we ought to answer each person (Col. 4:5-6).

There are clear marks of godly wisdom, the fruit of the genuine knowledge of God. Let us pray that God's people will more and more be distinguished, and our Lord honoured, by these good things: "The wisdom from above is first pure, then peaceable, gentle, open to reason, full of mercy and good fruits, impartial and sincere. And a harvest of righteousness is sown in peace by those who make peace" (James 3:17-18).

18. Paul Prays for Endurance for Believers

The Church around the world is sailing into a terrible storm, the worst it has ever seen or will see. This isn't the sort of storm that eventually blows itself out, leaving calm and normalcy in its wake. This rising tempest of antipathy and hatred against God, His Word, and His people will grow ever fiercer, I believe, until the end of the age.

Christians in the West, especially, who for many years have faced little true opposition or persecution, will increasingly find ourselves in need of a quality of character the Bible calls endurance. We will require God-given endurance in order to continue living in faithfulness to the Lord as the cost of doing so rises higher and higher.

The Bible repeatedly exhorts believers to endure, and commends them for doing so, on the implicit assumption that external conditions normally are not easy or favourable:

> *Patient endurance is what you need now, so that you will continue to do God's will. Then you will receive all that he has promised* (Hebrews 10:36).

> *Here is a trustworthy saying: If we died with him, we will also live with him; if we endure, we will also reign with him* (2 Timothy 2:12).

> *Consider him who endured such opposition from sinners, so that you will not grow weary and lose heart. In your struggle against sin, you have not yet resisted to the point of shedding your blood* (Hebrews 12:3-4).

> *I know all the things you do. I have seen your hard work and your patient endurance. I know*

you don't tolerate evil people. You have examined the claims of those who say they are apostles but are not. You have discovered they are liars. You have patiently suffered for me without quitting (Revelation 2:1-3 NLT).

But you, keep your head in all situations, endure hardship (2Timothy 4:5).

For God is pleased when, conscious of his will, you patiently endure unjust treatment. Of course, you get no credit for being patient if you are beaten for doing wrong. But if you suffer for doing good and endure it patiently, God is pleased with you (1 Peter 2:19 NLT).

For examples of patience in suffering, dear brothers and sisters, look at the prophets who spoke in the name of the Lord. We give great honour to those who endure under suffering. For instance, you know about Job, a man of great endurance. You can see how the Lord was kind to him at the end, for the Lord is full of tenderness and mercy (James 5:10-11 NLT).

Therefore, among God's churches we boast about your perseverance and faith in all the persecutions and trials you are enduring. All this is evidence that God's judgment is right, and as a result you will be counted worthy of the kingdom of God, for which you are suffering. God is just: He will pay back trouble to those who trouble you and give relief to you who are troubled, and to us as well. This will happen when the Lord Jesus is revealed from heaven in blazing fire with his powerful angels (2 Thess. 1:4-7).

Our source and great example of godly endurance is the Lord Himself. As we look to Him, He gives us grace to endure:

. . . let us run with endurance the race God has set before us. We do this by keeping our eyes on

Jesus, the champion who initiates and perfects our faith. Because of the joy awaiting him, he endured the cross, disregarding its shame. Now he is seated in the place of honour beside God's throne. Think of all the hostility he endured from sinful people; then you won't become weary and give up. After all, you have not yet given your lives in your struggle against sin (Hebrews 12:1-4 NLT).

Following Paul's example, we can and should pray for one another, that God would mightily strengthen us to endure whatever may come against us:

We continually ask God to fill you with the knowledge of his will through all the wisdom and understanding that the Spirit gives . . . being strengthened with all power according to his glorious might so that you may have great endurance and patience, and giving joyful thanks to the Father . . . (Colossians 1:9,11).

Christians often associate God's power and glorious might with signs, wonders and miracles. Some seem to seek these things from God to the exclusion of anything else. But there is a far more necessary and "enduring" manifestation of God's might in our lives, one that we would do far better to seek and have granted to us in this perilous hour. That is, supernatural endurance, that we may remain faithful, and persist in doing the will of God, in conditions that are certain to become ever more adverse as we approach the thunderous climax of history.

19. Paul Prays for the Fullness of Blessing for Believers

The prayers of the apostle Paul (see the appendix for a compilation of these wonderful prayers) reveal the marvellous, kind purposes of God for every one of His people. Whatever Paul asked for, we know that God desired then, and still desires now, to give to His children. This is absolutely vital to comprehend: Paul, inspired by the Holy Spirit, prayed for the saints according to the will of God. Paul's prayers express the will of God.

Paul's prayers also, when we give them serious thought, expose how far short of the fullness of God's blessings we tend to live. But let us not be overcome with dismay about this. The saints in Paul's day needed prayer, and so do we. Problem acknowledged. Now, let's learn what God wants to do in us and through us, and then pray in accordance with His will. As we see what the Lord wants to do, and as we ask Him to do it, He will work to fulfill His will and to answer our prayers.

In the prayers of Paul listed below, note how frequently the words "fill, full, and fullness" are used. And keep in mind that these fillings and fullnesses are God's will for His people in every generation. When Jesus said "I have come that they may have life, and have it to the full" (John 10:10), He surely meant these things above all else:

> *May the God of hope fill you with all joy and peace as you trust in him, so that you may overflow with hope by the power of the Holy Spirit* (Rom. 15:13).

And this is my prayer: that your love may abound more and more in knowledge and depth of insight, so that you may be able to discern what is best and may be pure and blameless until the day of Christ, filled with the fruit of righteousness that comes through Jesus Christ—to the glory and praise of God (Phil. 1:1-11).

For this reason, since the day we heard about you, we have not stopped praying for you and asking God to fill you with the knowledge of his will through all spiritual wisdom and understanding (Col. 1:9).

I want you to know how hard I am contending for you and for those at Laodicea, and for all who have not met me personally. My goal is that they may be encouraged in heart and united in love, so that they may have the full riches of complete understanding, in order that they may know the mystery of God, namely, Christ, in whom are hidden all the treasures of wisdom and knowledge (Col. 2:1-3).

I always thank my God as I remember you in my prayers, because I hear about your faith in the Lord Jesus and your love for all the saints. I pray that you may be active in sharing your faith, so that you will have a full understanding of every good thing we have in Christ (Philemon 1:4-6).

For this reason, ever since I heard about your faith in the Lord Jesus and your love for all the saints, I have not stopped giving thanks for you, remembering you in my prayers. I keep asking that the God of our Lord Jesus Christ, the glorious Father, may give you the Spirit of wisdom and revelation, so that you may know him better. I pray also that the eyes of your heart may be enlightened in order that you may know the hope to which he has called you, the riches of his glorious inheritance in the saints, and his incomparably great power for us who believe. That power is like the working of his mighty strength, which he exerted in Christ when he raised him from the dead and seated him at his right hand in the heavenly realms, far above all rule and authority, power and dominion, and every title that can be given, not only in the present age but also in the one to come. And God placed all things under his feet and appointed him to be head over everything for the church, which is his body, the fullness of him who fills everything in every way (Eph. 1:15-23).

And I pray that you, being rooted and established in love, may have power, together with all the saints, to grasp how wide and long and high and deep is the love of Christ, and to know this love that surpasses knowledge–that you may be filled to the measure of all the fullness of God. Now to him who is able to do immeasurably more than all we ask or imagine, according to his power that is at work within us, to him be glory in the church and in Christ Jesus throughout all generations, for ever and ever! Amen (Eph 3:18-21).

Yes, the Lord wants all of His people to be filled with all of His fullness! May He work in us to desire this as much as He does, and to seek Him for it as Paul did! If we will take God at His word, and ask Him, persistently, for the fullness that we know from Scripture that He desires for us to have, asking not only for ourselves but also for our brothers and sisters, then we will surely begin to receive and delight in that very fullness!

20. Paul Prays for Believers to be Filled With All God's Fullness

Abiding in Christ, and allowing Him and His Word to abide in us, is the open secret of Christian fruitfulness: "I am the vine; you are the branches. If you remain in me and I in you, you will bear much fruit; apart from me you can do nothing" (John 15:5). Jesus commended Mary for choosing "the one necessary thing," which was simply to come to Him in faith and receive from Him the words of life. As the Lord says repeatedly in Isaiah 55, "Come to me and listen carefully to me, and you shall live" (1-3). This is how believers maintain our vital connection with our only Source of life and fruit.

But coming to Jesus and listening to Him, keeping that connection with the Vine open so that His life may continually flow into us and through us, can be very hard. It isn't that it's hard to do physically or emotionally. It's no more difficult than settling into a comfortable chair and reading a novel or watching a movie. What can be hard, and sometimes very, very hard, is bringing ourselves to actually give appropriate time and attention to the Lord and His Word. How easy it is to give ourselves instead to the novel or the movie or the countless other diversions and distractions which unceasingly cry out for our time and attention.

Paul wrote of this universal, miserable human tendency: "For I do not do what I want, but I do the very thing I hate . . . For I have the desire to do what is right, but not the ability to carry it out.. . . O wretched man that I am!" (Romans 7). Regenerated, Spirit-baptized believers, even though we have a new nature in Christ, and all of the resources of Heaven at hand, continue to grapple with the choice between walking in the flesh and walking in the Spirit. And many of us, at many moments of decision, make wrong choices. Paul, knowing this fact of spiritual life, did not condemn believers for being weak. Instead, he prayed for them.

We all need the strength of the Holy Spirit to make right choices, especially to choose "the one necessary thing." The Lord is abundantly willing and able to give us this strength, through His Spirit, deep in our inner being. But it is clear that He would have us pray for one another for this overcoming strength. Why? Because, according to His perfect wisdom, our loving, effectual, edifying prayer for one another is an essential means of developing the character of Christ in both those who pray and those being prayed for.

Knowing this, Paul prayed for the Ephesian believers to receive the spiritual strength they needed in order to choose to allow Christ to abide in them:

For this reason I kneel before the Father, from whom every family in heaven and on earth derives its name. I pray that out of his glorious riches he may strengthen you with power through his Spirit in your inner being, so that Christ may dwell in your hearts through faith. And I pray that you, being rooted and established in love, may have power, together with all the Lord's holy people, to grasp how wide and long and high and deep is the love of Christ, and to know this love that surpasses knowledge—that you may be filled to the measure of all the fullness of God. Now to him who is able to do immeasurably more than all we ask or imagine, according to his power that is at work within us, to him be glory in the church and in Christ Jesus throughout all generations, for ever and ever! Amen (Eph. 3:14-21).

Paul's prayer is that the power of the Holy Spirit working deep in the Ephesians' hearts will overcome their tendency to draw back from God, and strengthen their desire to draw near to God and to live in nearness to Him. As this prayer unfolds, we see that abiding in Christ and His abiding in us ultimately produces tremendous understanding and experience of the love of Christ, and leads to being "filled to the measure of all the fullness of God." Paul's amazing prayer clearly reveals God's desire that we abide in Christ so that we can be filled with—and live in—all of His fullness.

Please note two things in connection with this prayer:

First, the experience of God's love and fullness is ultimately a communal blessing. We are to seek it not only for ourselves but for the whole Body, so that "together with all the Lord's holy people" we may grasp this love together. The true fullness of God's love cannot be grasped or comprehended, in fact, unless and until we love one another as He loves us. Such love is integral to the experience of God's fullness. In this prayer, Paul provides a clear and powerful example of the exercise of such love. Paul knows that glorious blessing awaits. He knows that weakness and obstacles stand in the way. So he prays, not for himself, but for the people of God, that together they would enter into the full possession of their inheritance in Christ.

Can we, twenty centuries later, pray in this way for one another? Certainly! Such prayer is very obviously according to the Word of God, and thus the will of God. The power to abide in Christ, and being filled with all of God's fullness, may seem too much to ask for, but they aren't. They are exactly what we should ask for. God inspired this prayer, because He earnestly wants us to have these blessings and would have us be aware of them, desire them, and seek them from Him.

Second, as great as this prayer is in its vision and desire for unspeakable blessing from God, the Lord is able to do much more! God can, and does, do far more than we can ask or imagine! Paul had received uncommon insight into the greatness of God and the power of His love. Paul was able to conceive of great blessing, and to seek for it. And yet, he knew that he had not comprehended everything that can be known of the fullness of God. However great Paul's conception of God and God's blessings, he understood that the full reality of God and His blessings is far greater. It is impossible to overstate the great goodness of God, who is far, far greater than our understanding of Him or any description of Him we may compose!

This prayer of Paul in Ephesians 3 is worthy of our prolonged, deep, receptive consideration. It is a glorious prayer that reveals God's wonderful intention for His people. We would do very well to make it a part of our own prayer lives. As we do, it will bless us and others in wonderful ways.

Lord, help us to take you at your word. It is your will to strengthen us so that we allow you to abide in us. It is your will for us, together with all of your people, to comprehend and experience the greatness of your love and the fullness of your Spirit. It is your will for us to have these glorious blessings, and for us to seek these blessings for one another. Please give us strength, understanding and love, so that we may desire and persistently seek these wonderful things that you greatly desire to bestow.

21. A Prayer for All Believers in All Circumstances

Each of us knows or knows of other believers for whom it can be especially hard to pray. That's because they're sinning. Or they're hypocrites. Or they've hurt us. Or we envy them. Or they're this, that or the other; we don't approve of who they are or what they're doing, and we're sure the Lord doesn't, either. So why should we pray for them? And how should we pray for them? "Lord, bless them"? No, we don't want the Lord to bless them, lest they become complacent in all the wrong they're doing.

But if they belong to God, then we owe them a debt of love. And we should pray for them. The apostle John writes, "If anyone sees his brother committing a sin not leading to death, he shall ask, and God will give him life—to those who commit sins that do not lead to death. There is sin that leads to death; I do not say that one should pray for that. All wrongdoing is sin, but there is sin that does not lead to death" (1 John 5:16-17).

The principle here is that our prayer can actually help restore believers to spiritual life who have fallen into sin and error. Our first impulse ought to be toward merciful restoration rather than condemnation. As James writes, "For judgment is without mercy to one who has shown no mercy. Mercy triumphs over judgment" (James 2:13).

This is not to say that sin and error must be tolerated or condoned. Far from it. But redeeming love must lie at the heart of Christian relationships and relating, even when confrontation, correction or discipline are required. And redeeming love in our hearts and our dealings, not coming naturally to us, must be sought at God's Throne of Grace.

In the book of Hebrews, there's a wonderful prayer which can be prayed for any believer, whatever their need, weakness or sin. It can be prayed safely and confidently in all circumstances, especially when we don't know exactly what the problem is or where the answer lies: "May the God of peace, who through the blood of the eternal covenant brought back from the dead our Lord Jesus, that great Shepherd of the sheep, equip you with everything good for doing his will, and may he work in us what is pleasing to him, through Jesus Christ, to whom be glory for ever and ever. Amen" (Hebrews 13:20-21).

"May He work in us what is pleasing to Him, through Jesus Christ." Note several facets of this excellent prayer:

1. It assures us that it is possible to please God and that He earnestly desires to be pleased with us. Some people seem to believe that God enjoys simmering in constant anger toward His people, but such a notion is blasphemous. This prayer recalls the glorious promise, "for it is God who works in you, both to will and to work for his good pleasure" (Philippians 2:13).

2. It completely relinquishes any attempt to impose our own wishes, ambition or agenda upon the ones for whom we are praying. It is a prayer utterly devoid of human manipulation and meddling. It seeks God's will and pleasure, not ours.

3. It trusts the Lord, who alone knows what is best, to do what is best.

4. It places no limits on God, affirming that He can work the impossible, even with "impossible" people.

5. It allows us to pray wholeheartedly and with love for others, no matter how we feel about them or what the circumstances, knowing that what is pleasing to the Lord cannot be anything but the best, and the wisest, and the most greatly to be desired of all possible outcomes.

6. Its "us" includes those praying as also needing God's great transforming work. The fact that others may have weaknesses and needs does not mean that we do not.

7. It can be prayed for all saints alike, whether they are victorious or struggling. There is no Christian or group of Christians for whom it is not always an appropriate prayer. But it is ideal for those "caught in any transgression," whom those who are spiritual should "restore in a spirit of gentleness," minding themselves lest they too be tempted. It is a prayer that helps bear the burdens of others, fulfilling the law of Christ (Galatians 6:1-2).

Lord, please work in us and in all of your people what is pleasing to You. Nothing is more to be desired than this. And open our hearts to comprehend and believe that what is pleasing to You, concerning us, is nothing less than glorious.

22. Paul Prays for the Salvation of Israel

The apostle Paul cared deeply for his fellow Jews who had rejected their Messiah: "I speak the truth in Christ—I am not lying, my conscience confirms it through the Holy Spirit—I have great sorrow and unceasing anguish in my heart. For I could wish that I myself were cursed and cut off from Christ for the sake of my people, those of my own race, the people of Israel" (Romans 9:1-4). Yearning for his kinsmen, Paul prayed: "Brothers, my heart's desire and prayer to God for them is that they may be saved" (Romans 10: 1).

Paul knew that such prayer would receive an answer, that Israel would eventually turn to Jesus. He wrote to the Gentile believers in Rome: "Lest you be wise in your own sight, I do not want you to be unaware of this mystery, brothers: a partial hardening has come upon Israel, until the fullness of the Gentiles has come in. And in this way all Israel will be saved, as it is written, 'The Deliverer will come from Zion, he will banish ungodliness from Jacob'; 'and this will be my covenant with them when I take away their sins'" (Romans 11:25-27).

This has much to do with God's plan for the Church. Paul calls Gentile believers to remember that we were once "alienated from the commonwealth of Israel and strangers to the covenants of promise, having no hope and without God in the world. But now in Christ Jesus you who once were far off have been brought near by the blood of Christ. For he himself is our peace, who has made us both one and has broken down in his flesh the dividing wall of hostility by abolishing the law of commandments expressed in ordinances, that he might create in himself one new man in place of the two, so making peace, and might reconcile us both to

God in one body through the cross, thereby killing the hostility" (Eph. 2:12-16).

The separated "two" made one new man in Christ are Jew and Gentile. No longer strangers, we are fellow-members of the family of God. Together, we are the Body of Christ, being built into a holy dwelling place for God by the Holy Spirit. The Church which Jesus promised to build, and to present to Himself as a glorious Bride, must include some large number of Jewish believers. Most of these have yet to believe in Christ, and until they do, the Body cannot be complete.

Christians therefore ought to pray, as Paul did, for the salvation of Israel. And we ought to extend mercy to Israel and the Jews as we have opportunity, for they are "beloved for the sake of their forefathers" (Romans 11:28). Much harm has been done to Jews "in the name of Christ" that needs to be overcome. Many hundreds of years of Christian anti-Semitism, which sadly continues to this very day, have made it difficult for Jews even to consider the truth about their Messiah. It is a gracious miracle of God every time a Jew turns to Christ—something which, thankfully, is happening more and more.

Let us rejoice in the rebirth of Israel in 1948. This amazing event, foretold by prophets, apostles and Jesus Himself, is mighty, irrefutable evidence, presented openly before the whole world, of the inerrant truth of Scripture, of the absolute faithfulness of God to His promises, and of the glorious mercy of God toward undeserving sinners. Let not Gentile Christians, foolishly "wise in their own sight," disparage that which God in His merciful kindness has done for Israel, nor remain ignorant of that which He yet intends to do. For one day, "all Israel will be saved," and the truly wise can have a part in helping that to happen.

God is working in Israel and among the Jews. Like Elijah's "cloud the size of a man's hand," something miraculous and wonderful is forming on Israel's spiritual horizon. For an example of how very smart, very courageous Messianic Israelis are reaching Jews in Israel and around the world for Christ—and to help them in this wonderful work—visit One for Israel *https://www.oneforisrael.org/.* Their guiding conviction: **"Because the best way to bless Israel is with Jesus."**

23. Paul Commends Epaphras, a Praying Man

Epaphras was a believer from Colossae, a city near Laodicea in Asia Minor. He was evidently a founder of the church there, having preached the gospel to his fellow Colossians. For a time, he traveled and ministered with the apostle Paul. He was also imprisoned with Paul in Rome (Philemon 23), from whence the letter to the Colossians was sent. Paul calls Epaphras "our dear fellow servant, who is a faithful minister of Christ on our behalf . . . " (Col 1:7).

At the close of the letter, Paul mentions Epaphras again: "Epaphras, who is one of you and a servant of Christ Jesus, sends greetings. He is always wrestling in prayer for you, that you may stand firm in all the will of God, mature and fully assured. I vouch for him that he is working hard for you and for those in Laodicea and and Hierapolis" (Col 4:12-13).

Paul's references to Epaphras are brief but laden with truth and significance. The apostle's warm commendation, "a dear fellow servant, who is a faithful minister of Christ," can be taken as coming from the Holy Spirit Himself. What more welcome assessment could a believer receive from God? In fact, this, precisely, is what we all hope to hear when we reach the end of our journey: "Well done, good and faithful servant."

It is noteworthy that Epaphras, like Paul, seems unconcerned about the injustice of his imprisonment. There is no record here of defence lawyers, demonstrations, letter-writing campaigns, protests or hunger strikes demanding release. It wasn't that these men wouldn't have much preferred to be at liberty. As Paul had written to bondservants among the Corinthians, "But if you can gain your freedom, avail yourself of the opportunity." But since they have been imprisoned for Christ's sake, they are content to serve Him in their bonds.

Indeed, although constrained bodily, Epaphras is free in the Spirit. And what great use he makes of this liberty! Far more concerned with the welfare of his brothers and sisters back home than about his own plight, he earnestly prays for them. He prays for them continually and, no doubt following Paul's example, according to the will of God:

1. That the believers would stand—that they would not fall and would not fail

2. That they would stand firm—that they would not draw back from God, would not compromise the truth of the Gospel, would not buckle under pressure but would hold unswervingly to the hope they professed

3. That they would stand firm in the will of God—steadfast and immovable, abounding in the work of the Lord, knowing that their labour in the Lord was not in vain

4. That they would become spiritually mature—wise, loving, discerning, fruitful, and walking in holiness and unity

5. That they would become fully assured—not up one day and down the next, doubting God's love for them, but living in steady, joyful confidence of their acceptance and adoption through Christ

On the basis of his companion's faithful, continual prayer, Paul says of Epaphras, "I vouch for him that he is working hard for you and for those in Laodicea and and Hierapolis." Again, this is tantamount to commendation from God Himself. The Lord takes approving notice of faithful, edifying, persistent prayer for His beloved people. He sees it as obedience to His commandment that we love one another, and He finds great pleasure in it.

Many believers today are facing physical constraints, whether due to the coronavirus, to ill health, to advanced age, or to all three. Whatever our physical circumstances, every believer has the liberty and confidence, through the blood of Christ, to "draw near to the throne of grace, that we may receive mercy and find grace to help in time of need" (Hebrews 4:16). So, may the Lord strengthen us to faithfully and persistently do this very thing, praying not only for ourselves, but also for our brothers and sisters. Like Epaphras, may we be found to be faithful ministers of Christ, working hard for one another in prayer, that we may stand firm in all the will of God, mature and fully assured!

24. Paul on the Purpose of Ministry

In Ephesians 4, Paul lays out God's plan for the Church, and how it is to be accomplished:

And He [Jesus] gave the apostles, the prophets, the evangelists, the shepherds [pastors] and teachers, to equip the saints for the work of ministry, for building up the body of Christ, until we all attain to the unity of the faith and of the knowledge of the Son of God, to mature manhood, to the measure of the stature of the fullness of Christ, so that we may no longer be children, tossed to and fro by the waves and carried about by every wind of doctrine, by human cunning, by craftiness in deceitful schemes. Rather, speaking the truth in love, we are to grow up in every way into Him who is the head, into Christ, from whom the whole body, joined and held together by every joint with which it is equipped, when each part is working properly, makes the body grow so that it builds itself up in love. (Eph. 4:11-16).

God's plan for His people, the Church, the Body of Christ, is that we grow toward full maturity and completeness in Him, preparing to become His pure, radiant Bride in a glorious spiritual union with Him that will never end.

This plan of God is unfolding today and every day, in a process which encompasses all true believers everywhere on earth. While God is sovereignly directing, inspiring and empowering this process, He is also using us, the members of His Body, to bring it to pass. It is not so much a process that happens "to us," as one which happens "in us" and "through us." It is a process which, according to God's excellent wisdom, requires our willing, wise participation. The more willingly and wisely each of us does our part, "working properly" as Paul puts it, the fuller the growth the Body will experience. The less commitment there is among the members of the Body to edify one another, the less edification the Body will see. The condition of the Body at any stage in its history, including in this present day, is very much a function of the degree to which the members "work properly" to edify one another in love.

How are the members of the Body to "work properly?" How does that happen? According to our passage in Ephesians 4, they are to be equipped (trained, taught) to do so. The passage clearly states that God has given "gifts" to the Church in order to accomplish this equipping. These gifts are human ministers: apostles, prophets, evangelists, shepherds (pastors) and teachers.

The apostles and prophets came first, laying the fixed foundation of the spoken revelation of God upon which all subsequent building and growth arises. From the beginning of the Church, evangelists have been given, preaching the Good News and calling all who will hear it out of the world into saving faith in Christ. And from the beginning, in every congregation of the true church, the Lord has given pastor-teachers to feed and protect His newly-born lambs and His flocks. According to Ephesians 4, the primary calling and duty of ministers gifted by Christ to the Church has been to equip (train, teach) the people of God to edify the people of God for the glory of God. And, of course, the training syllabus is the Word of God, the Bible.

"Edification" is growing up into Christ, through a process of learning, of reception of Bible truth. Being edified means learning about Christ, learning to seek Christ, learning to put on Christ, learning to trust and obey Christ, learning to serve Christ and, above all, learning to know and love Christ. That is why mature believers, by definition, are "no longer children, tossed to and fro by the waves and carried about by every wind of doctrine, by human cunning, by craftiness in deceitful schemes." Mature believers, by definition, have received sufficient truth that they are able to discern, avoid and oppose that which is not truth.

Mature believers also, by definition, must desire and labour that their brothers and sisters may grow up into Christ. The process of coming to maturity must include assuming one's responsibility to help build up the Body in love. This is what true ministers equip believers to do. The believer who has no interest in or puts no effort into edifying the Body is, by definition, immature. The only way for the Body to come to maturity is for each of us to understand and fulfill our calling to help build up the Body in love. And for this, according to Ephesians 4, we need the teaching and example of God-sent ministers.

It is a sad reality that, in the Church today, or at least among those who profess Christ, there are many "ministers" who, instead of carrying out the charge to equip the saints to become mature, are keeping their followers in a constant state of immaturity. There are a number of possible reasons for this. Some ministers may be too immature themselves to understand what their calling really is. Meaning well, they distract and busy God's people with projects and visions of their own imagining. Some may not want to share the exalted work of ministry with "ordinary" believers. Some, knowing that immature believers are relatively easy to manipulate and rule, may prefer an immature, compliant flock to a well-taught, discerning one. Some may be propagating winds of false doctrine and want no accountability or opposition. Or some may be operating, for their own gain, cunning and crafty schemes. It is hardly a secret that in all the world there are perhaps no more gullible and vulnerable marks, or targets of deception, than sincere but immature Christians.

"Ministers" who are motivated by anything other than love for Christ, and the desire to call unbelievers to Him and believers to maturity and fullness in Him, may assume all sorts of titles, but they are not Christ's gifts to the Church. And Christians should not follow them.

As part of our "working properly" to help edify the Body of Christ, let us ask the Lord to send true shepherds who will fulfill the scriptural charge to "equip the saints for the work of ministry, for building up the Body of Christ" so that we can grow toward maturity and unity in Christ, and glorify Him greatly. And let us thank the Lord for the many He has given. These are God's gifts to His people, to be appreciated, supported and encouraged.

25. Paul's Persistence in Prayer

In the parable of the man who went to his friend at midnight, Jesus teaches that effectual prayer requires persistence. The man kept knocking on the door until the friend got out of bed and gave him as much bread as he needed. The Lord explains: "Though he will not rise and give to him because he is his friend, yet because of his persistence he will rise and give him as much as he needs. So I say to you, ask, and it will be given to you; seek, and you will find; knock, and it will be opened to you. For everyone who asks receives, and he who seeks finds, and to him who knocks it will be opened. If a son asks for bread from any father among you, will he give him a stone? Or if he asks for a fish, will he give him a serpent instead? Or if he asks for an egg, will he offer him a scorpion? If you then, being evil, know how to give good gifts to your children, how much more will your heavenly Father give the Holy Spirit to those who ask Him!" (Luke 11:8-13 NKJ).

How important it is to press in and press on in pursuit of God and His blessings! We may have very good understanding of God's will for His people. We may be well aware of the heavenly riches the Lord stands abundantly ready to pour out upon the Church (the chief of which, according to verse 13, is His very self, through the Holy Spirit). But we must set ourselves to seek God tenaciously in order to receive that which He has promised.

Is this because God is reluctant to bless? Absolutely not. He is far more willing to give than we are to receive. But, just as by subjecting us to the very necessity of prayer itself, in His perfect wisdom He works eternal good for us by cultivating persistence in our prayer. We may not fully understand or concur with God's ways, but we have no fruitful option but to believe His clear teaching and submit ourselves to it. He sets all of the terms and conditions for living in His Kingdom.

This may seem like hard news to those who are already exhausted at the thought of prayer, much less of persistent prayer. I would encourage those who may feel this way to reread Chapter 1, "The Wellspring of Effectual Prayer." Like every good thing in our lives, the inclination and power to persist in prayer are a fruit of connection to Jesus the Vine. What may seem impossible to the natural mind is not only possible as the life of Christ fills us, it can become the great delight of our lives.

Also, we must be sure that what we are seeking in prayer is according to the will and Word of God. No amount of persistence in asking amiss is going to produce answers. As I explained in earlier chapters, I believe the will of God is above all else to bring all of His people to sanctification, maturity and fullness in Christ. Our heavenly Father is very pleased to hear prayers that persistently seek these things, and I believe He will answer them in wonderful ways in due season.

I would caution here against trying to set up, consciously or subconsciously, any legalistic standard by which to assess one's persistence in prayer. Persistence is a fruit of abiding in Christ, and, like natural fruit, the result of a process of growth. The Lord says "Take my yoke upon you," but He also says, "My yoke is easy and my burden is light" (Matthew 11:29-30). Persistence is not so much a function of marathon prayer sessions, but of keeping your heart on the objective and asking, seeking and knocking as you are reasonably able. What you know God wills, keep going back to in prayer. Don't give Him rest. Never give up.

Consider Elijah after the rout of the prophets of Baal. Following years of drought in Israel, the prophet now perceived, prophetically, the approach of "an abundance of rain." Elijah knew that God was going to give rain. But he also knew that God wanted him to ask for that rain. So he went up to the top of Mount Carmel and set himself to pray: "And he bowed himself down on the earth and put his face between his knees. And he said to his servant, 'Go up now, look toward the sea.' And he went up and looked and said, 'There is nothing.' And he said, 'Go again,' seven times."

One, two, three, four, five, six times, after periods of prayer, Elijah sent his servant to look out over the Mediterranean for some sign of rain, but there was nothing to see. The seventh time was different. The servant came back and said, "'Behold, a little cloud like a man's hand is rising from the sea.' . . . And in a little while the heavens grew black with clouds and wind, and there was a great rain" (1 Kings 18:42-45).

What great lessons we can learn from this episode! Elijah knew that God was going send rain. But Elijah had to seek God for it. And he had to seek it persistently. He had to continue seeking until the answer came. The answer was almost imperceptible at first. But then, finally, God opened the heavens and released a great, refreshing, life-giving downpour of rain!

I believe that the Church is in dire need of a life-giving visitation of God's Spirit and deeper dedication to His Word. I believe that God greatly desires to answer our need and fill His people with all of His fullness. He has declared that He will build His Church, and that He will bring us to maturity and fullness so that the world will receive glorious witness of His great love. He has shown us what He wills and how to ask Him for it. Now, like Elijah, we must ask our Father to do what He has said He will do. And, like Elijah, we must ask, seek and knock, persistently, until the Lord does what He said He will do!

We can take encouragement from the apostle James: "The prayer of a righteous person is powerful and effective. Elijah was a human being, even as we are. He prayed earnestly that it would not rain, and it did not rain on the land for three and a half years. Again he prayed, and the heavens gave rain, and the earth produced its crops" (5:16-18).

We can take encouragement also from the apostle Paul, who prayed according to the will of God with great persistence, and bore much fruit for the glory of God. May the Lord work something of Paul's loving persistence in prayer into our lives:

> *God, whom I serve with my whole heart in preaching the gospel of his Son, is my witness how constantly I remember you in my prayers at all times . . .* (Rom. 1:9-10).

> *For this reason, ever since I heard about your faith in the Lord Jesus and your love for all the saints, I have not stopped giving thanks for you, remembering you in my prayers. I keep asking . . .* (Eph. 1:15-17).

> *And pray in the Spirit on all occasions with all kinds of prayers and requests. With this in mind, be alert and always keep on praying for all the saints* (Eph. 6:18).

> *For this reason, since the day we heard about you, we have not stopped praying for you and asking God to fill you with the knowledge of his will through all spiritual wisdom and under-standing* (Col. 1:9).

> *Epaphras, who is one of you and a servant of Christ Jesus, sends greetings. He is always wrestling in prayer for you, that you may stand firm in all the will of God, mature and fully assured* (Col. 4:12).

> *How can we thank God enough for you in return for all the joy we have in the presence of our God because of you? Night and day we pray most earnestly that we may see you again and supply what is lacking in your faith* (1Thess. 3:9-10).

Be joyful always; pray continually . . .
(1Thess. 5:16-17).

With this in mind, we constantly pray for you, that our God may count you worthy of his calling, and that by his power he may fulfill every good purpose of yours and every act prompted by your faith (2 Thess. 1:11).

I thank God, whom I serve, as my forefathers did, with a clear conscience, as night and day I constantly remember you in my prayers
(2 Tim. 1:3).

By faith, can you hear the sound of an abundance of spiritual rain? If so, then ask, and keep asking, until we see God's desire and Word fulfilled!

26. Abraham's Faith and Edifying Prayer

In Romans 4, Paul explains how Abraham is the father of all the faithful, both Jew and Gentile. Because he believed what God said to him, Abraham was credited with righteousness:

> . . . the word of the LORD came to Abram in a vision: 'Do not be afraid, Abram. I am your shield, your very great reward.'
> But Abram replied, 'O Lord GOD, what can You give me, since I remain childless, and the heir of my house is Eliezer of Damascus?' Abram continued, 'Behold, You have given me no offspring, so a servant in my household will be my heir.'
> Then the word of the LORD came to Abram, saying, 'This one will not be your heir, but one who comes from your own body will be your heir.' And the LORD took him outside and said, 'Now look to the heavens and count the stars, if you are able.' Then He told him, 'So shall your offspring be.'
> Abram believed the LORD, and it was credited to him as righteousness (Genesis 15:1-6).

Abraham understood that the fulfillment of all of the great promises of God to him depended, first of all, upon him and Sarah having a son, "one who comes from your own body." So let's consider for a moment the relationship between faith and works or action in the life of Abraham and Sarah.

When Abraham believed God upon hearing the promise in Genesis 15, "it was credited to him as righteousness." This was an instantaneous imputation of righteousness by grace, through the hearing of faith, and not through works.

But before the patriarch could begin to see the fulfillment of God's promise to give him an heir and make him the father of many nations, he had to act on his faith in God. He and Sarah both had to act in faith. Abraham knew that faith did not entail waiting for his promised son to be supernaturally conceived by the Holy Spirit in the womb of Sarah (the way Jesus was conceived in the womb of Mary).

For Abraham to merely wait for God to do what He had promised to do would have been vain and fruitless presumption, not an exercise of faith. True faith required Abraham and Sarah to do what they knew needed to be done whenever a man and woman wish to have a child: to have sexual relations. The conception of Isaac, although it was miraculous in that God ensured that it happened in spite of the couple's advanced age and Sarah's prior infertility, was a normal conception in the sense that it resulted from their intercourse and the joining of Abraham's seed and Sarah's egg.

This meant that, over the long period of time between the son being promised and Isaac being conceived, Abraham and Sarah had to persist in exercising their faith in God's promise by repeatedly having intercourse in the hope of conceiving. We do not know, and do not need to know, how often they did this. We can assume that it wasn't always easy (nor was it mere drudgery!) for them to keep trusting God, and we know that they became discouraged at times. We know that they made a huge mistake when they tried to make a surrogate of Hagar, resulting in the birth of Ishmael.

But God corrected and encouraged Abraham and Sarah, and they continued on in faith and hope. We know that they continued doing what they know was necessary if they were ever to have a son. And eventually, wonderfully, just as the Lord had promised,

Isaac was conceived and born, when Abraham was 100 years old.

What this means to us, in the context of Christian life in general and prayer in particular, is that God's promises to us—unless He tells us otherwise—rarely come to fulfillment without the exercise of faith, through appropriate action, on our part.

We have promises from the Lord that He will build His church. Jesus prayed for this to happen. He gave His life for it to happen. He ascended on high and gave ministry gifts to the Church in order to equip her members to do the work of building up the Body of Christ (see Chapter 24) until we reach "mature manhood, the measure of the stature of the fullness of Christ" (Eph. 4:13). And He gave all of us the privilege and responsibility of praying, labouring with Christ in this great work of edifying one another in love.

We know that the Lord is building His Church. But we cannot presume to "leave it up to Him," any more than Abraham and Sarah could presume ever to see the birth of their promised son without doing what it takes to have a child. God does not want His Church to drift aimlessly, waiting for some sudden miraculous deliverance from countless enemies and from our own apathy, worldliness, division, weakness and error. Such a "faith," without our works, is dead.

The Lord wants us to take hold of His promises and to call upon Him, according to His Word, that He do what we know He desires to do and has promised to do and has sacrificed His life to do—to "present the church to Himself in splendour, without spot or wrinkle or any such thing, that she might be holy and without blemish" (Eph 5:27).

The Lord would have each of us arise and build. It is only through the very processes and acts of edifying one another in love, according to His Word and through His Spirit, that we can come to maturity in Christ. None of us can afford to sit this out.

27. Being Strong Through Prayer for One Another

Paul closes his epistle to the Ephesians with the exhortation, "Finally, be strong in the Lord and in His mighty power" (Eph. 6:10). He then enumerates the "armour of God," well-known to many Christians and the subject of numerous sermons and books. Putting on the whole armour of God is indeed crucial to standing strong in the Lord. It is necessary. But, according to the passage, it is not sufficient.

After listing the armour, but continuing with his "be strong" exhortation, Paul also urges believers to pray:

And pray in the Spirit on all occasions with all kinds of prayers and requests. With this in mind, be alert and always keep on praying for all the saints. Pray also for me, that whenever I open my mouth, words may be given me so that I will fearlessly make known the mystery of the gospel, for which I am an ambassador in chains. Pray that I may declare it fearlessly, as I should (v. 18-20).

The logic and syntax of the whole "be strong" exhortation indicate that prayer, as much as the spiritual armour, is a vital part of being strong in the Lord.

More to the point, it is "praying for all the saints" that enables us to be strong in the Lord. "With this in mind," that is, being aware of the spiritual battle we are all fighting, we must pray for one another. Why is all-inclusive prayer for the saints so important? First, because all of God's people are one Body. If one member suffers, we all suffer. If one member fails, that failure hurts the whole Body. So we should pray for all of God's people, holding them up before the Throne of Grace. To the natural mind, it may seem ludicrous to

94

pray for many millions of people we don't even know, but I believe the Lord can teach us to do this in such a way that it pleases Him and edifies the Body.

Secondly, and perhaps more importantly, "praying for all the saints" means praying for those believers we do know who have offended or annoyed us, with whom we disagree, or whom we do not like. In order to be strong in the Lord, we must pray, with love, for such people—especially for such people!

What happens if we do not pray for Christians we dislike or resent? Our spiritual enemies gain an advantage over us. Allowing ill will toward any other believer to linger in our hearts, without truly and lovingly seeking their good in prayer, is plain disobedience to the Lord. Such lack of forgiving love will manifest itself in criticism, gossip, backbiting and every sort of conflict. In extreme cases, it can cause mental and emotional damage. And it will always result in spiritual weakness in us as individuals, and in the Body.

If, on the other hand, we pray for all believers, especially those (and we all know such, don't we?) for whom we don't really want to pray, we help to strengthen the Body and to defeat the wiles of our true spiritual enemies. Praying for our brothers and sisters, particularly the "problematic" ones, in obedience to the Lord, makes us stronger in Him and opens a way to victory in both their lives and ours.

This is not to say that if there has been offence or error we should do nothing about it but pray. Scripture does not teach "do nothing about it but pray." Substituting prayer for proper biblical response to offence and error is often simply cowardice in disguise. But when there has been offence or error, when there is conflict among believers, truly loving prayer is essential to handling it well, and will help bring forth a resolution that is pleasing to God and edifying for all concerned.

Praying for all God's people, seeking the fullness of God's blessing for them and desiring to see them stand pure, blameless and joyful "on that Day," is love in action. It pleases the Lord, who said, "This is my command, that you love one another" (John 15:12). Such prayer will guard our hearts and minds. It will help prevent us from doing or saying things, in the heat of conflict, which offend the Lord, hurt the Body, and give place to the enemy. According to the apostle Paul, such prayer will help us to "be strong in the Lord, and in His mighty power."

Is there a believer you really, really don't want to pray for? Perhaps he or she is coming to mind right now, and the very thought of them causes you pain. That is the one you really must pray for, with the sincere love which bears all things and hopes all things (1 Cor. 13). Might you ask the Lord to give you the grace to pray effectually for that one? Your spiritual health and strength, and that of the Body, in some measure depend on it.

Please note Paul exhorts us to "always keep on praying for all the saints." *Persistence* in prayer for *all* of God's people is an absolutely vital element of staying strong in the Lord. We must never quit, because perseverance and persistence in such prayer brings continual personal victory and the certainty of glorious answers, from the Lord, among His people. There never comes a point in this present life at which we may lay down the blessed yoke of edifying prayer.

A final key detail in this passage is that Paul also requests prayer for himself. It isn't really prayer for himself, or in his own self-interest, but rather for the work of preaching the Gospel and edifying the Church. He asks for prayer that, whenever he preaches or teaches, the Lord will give him both words to say and courage to say them without fear or compromise.

I believe we can apply Paul's request for prayer and the principle behind it to those in Gospel ministry in our day. The Church, and the world, need to hear courageous, fearless preaching of God-given messages. Believers must go beyond merely lamenting "the weak condition of the Church today and the poor quality of preaching." (Indeed, there is in fact much excellent teaching and preaching ministry in the Church today.) Where there is need, we can, and must, strengthen the Church and its Gospel proclamation through loving, persistent, edifying prayer.

28. When Prayer Goes Up, God's Fire Comes Down

More and more, I am seeing very distressing reports of persecution, corruption and apostasy in Christendom. The Church has always been under siege, but it seems as if every conceivable (and inconceivable!) weapon of wickedness is being launched against it in this hour.

The most painful and dismaying reports are not those of external persecution of Christians for their commitment to Christ and the Gospel. Such things we ought to expect and we can actually rejoice in. The most damaging problems are failures and corruptions within the Church, which bring reproach to Christ, scorn upon His Body, and discouragement among His people. The very worst of these offences involve leaders who lie against the truth while abusing, exploiting or misleading God's sheep. Parts of the Church are in need of deep cleansing, purging, sanctification. This the Lord will undertake as we earnestly seek Him for it.

Consider John's vision of God's throne in Heaven: "And when He had taken the scroll, the four living creatures and the twenty-four elders fell down before the Lamb, each holding a harp, and golden bowls full of incense, which are the prayers of the saints" (Rev. 5:8). We need to understand that our effectual, fervent prayers rise as incense before the throne of God in Heaven. It is certain that our prayers reach the Lord and that He takes notice of them. And, to the extent that they seek His glory and the fulfillment of His will, He answers them. A little further along, John writes:

And another angel came and stood at the altar with a golden censer, and he was given much incense to offer with the prayers of all the saints on the golden altar before the throne, and the smoke of the incense, with the prayers of the saints, rose before God from the hand of the angel. Then the angel took the censer and filled it with fire from the altar and threw it on the earth, and there were peals of thunder, rumblings, flashes of lightning, and an earthquake (Rev. 8:3-5).

In this heavenly scene, the saints seek justice against wicked oppressors. Their prayers ascend before the throne of the Almighty. God responds by sending fire down upon the earth. In the same way, as we earnestly seek God to cleanse His Church of that which offends Him and harms His people, He will indeed send fire down. He is highly displeased with Christians and supposed Christians, especially leaders, who exploit His sheep or lead them astray.

This fire of God upon His Church is not a physical phenomenon, of course. It comes at first as a fiery conviction of sin, an intense inner urging by the Holy Spirit to obey the Word and repent. God's desire is for sinners to repent quickly and to be cleansed, forgiven and restored. If His conviction is resisted, however, it becomes a fire of illumination, of light shining into dark places and exposing hidden sin to others. With this fire can come the intense pain of shame, trouble and personal loss. If repentance is still resisted, God's fire eventually becomes a fire of judgement. As Jesus said of "Jezebel," a corrupt influencer in the church of Thyatira: "I gave her time to repent, but she refuses to repent of her sexual immorality. Behold, I will throw her onto a sickbed, and those who commit adultery with her I will throw into great tribulation, unless they repent of her works, and I will strike her children dead" (Rev. 2:21-23).

God's dealing with serious sin is serious business, but it is necessary and, among whatever segments of the Church there may be that are careless, lukewarm and permissive, long past due. "For it is time for judgment to begin at the household of God; and if it begins with us, what will be the outcome for those who do not obey the gospel of God?" (1 Peter 4:17). Only when idols and wickedness are put away from among God's people can we expect the fullness of His presence and blessing.

Let us not merely deplore and bemoan gross sin and error in the Church. Let us also pray that the Word and Spirit of God will find deep entrance and bring sanctifying, transforming conviction upon the people of God. In response, the Lord will indeed send His cleansing fire upon us. This fire will do no harm to those who are pure in heart, but rather stir in them righteous indignation, courage and conviction to confront evil in the Church and to overcome it. Lord, let your cleansing fire fall!

29. The Holy Spirit Also Intercedes for Believers

Paul writes that all of creation, including the people of God, is groaning with longing for the resurrection and for the deliverance of the universe from death and decay. And "In the same way," he says, "the Spirit helps us in our weakness. We do not know what we ought to pray for, but the Spirit himself intercedes for us through wordless groans. And he who searches our hearts knows the mind of the Spirit, because the Spirit intercedes for God's people in accordance with the will of God" (Romans 8:26-27).

This passage is profoundly encouraging. The very Spirit of God is seeking our good at all times, with a love and empathy which transcend language. After all, words are but signifiers of things, not the things themselves. When it comes to the deep things of God, words fail. Words alone are incapable of conveying the full reality of that which they signify.

This passage is not saying that we never know anything about what we should pray for. Such an interpretation would contradict the many other passages of Scripture, including the prayers of Paul, which tell us quite clearly what we ought to pray for. So it isn't that we're completely ignorant. But our knowledge and understanding are always incomplete, and our faith and motivation are always imperfect. So the Holy Spirit, whose knowledge and love are perfect, graciously helps us in several ways.

First, we and the Church always have needs that we may not even be aware of. But God sees all and knows all. So even when we are ignorant of our need or someone else's, the Holy Spirit is helping us by making intercession for us.

Then there are situations in which there is a need about which we know we should pray, but we do not know the precise nature of the need or what the best answer to it may be. In such situations, we can be confident that the Holy Spirit knows exactly what the true nature of the problem is and what the best answer is. This passage assures us that, in spite of our weakness, the Holy Spirit intercedes for us with the Father in order to "work all things together for good" for those who love the Lord.

Finally, even when we do have a reasonably clear idea of what the will of God is, and thus what we should pray for, our words alone may not be sufficient to convey the full nature of either the need or of the answer that will meet the need. For example, Paul prayed, as we ought also to pray, that marvellous prayer in Ephesians 3 that God's people may "be filled with all of the fullness of God" (Eph. 3:19). We have some understanding of what these words mean when we read them and when we pray them. And it is good to meditate on these words and to pray them with all of our hearts, knowing that it is the will of God to fill us with His fullness.

But the true and complete sense of what it is to be "filled with all of the fullness of God"? We can barely begin to conceive of it except the Lord reveal it to us. The reality goes beyond words, just as "the love of Christ which surpasses knowledge" cannot be fully comprehended in human speech or even in human experience. But the Holy Spirit, who is God and who fully knows and lovingly seeks the will of God for us, is able to comprehend exactly, and express precisely, through wordless groans, our overwhelming, unutterable need and longing to be filled with the very fullness of God.

So it is with many of the deep issues and unspeakable blessings of Christian life, of which mere words simply cannot carry the full meaning and significance. The Holy Spirit knows all things, and the Father fully knows the mind of the Spirit, and they work together in all things for our good, answering the deep,

deep needs in our lives—the needs which we, being frail creatures, lack the capacity and even the desire to express adequately.

30. Every Believer's Call to Build with Christ

Jesus promised, "I will build my church, and the gates of hell shall not prevail against it" (Matthew 16:18). We can be confident that, throughout the ebb and flow and ups and downs of Church history, the Lord has been working to fulfill that promise. We can trust Him for the future also: "He who began a good work in you will carry it on to completion until the day of Christ Jesus" (Phil. 1:6).

But we must also recognize that God has ordained that believers share a large responsibility in the building of the Church. According to His excellent wisdom, the Lord builds the Church through the Church, by teaching and empowering its members to edify one another in love. When we are paying attention to Him and obeying Him, the Church experiences a self-edifying virtuous cycle:

As we are edified, we grow "into Christ," knowing Him more and more, and becoming more like Him. And then we grow "from Christ," as mutual love and edification increasingly flow out of our growing connection with Him: "Speaking the truth in love, we are to grow up in every way into him who is the head, into Christ, from whom the whole body, joined and held together by every joint with which it is equipped, when each part is working properly, makes the body grow so that it builds itself up in love" (Eph. 4:15-16).

The Body's full maturity in Christ will be attained when all of its members become devoted to edifying one another in love. I do not expect a miraculous, instantaneous shortcut that will produce this state. I believe there must instead be persistent learning and growth toward our promised maturity.

God's will is that all the members of His Body learn to love and edify one another. It is only as each of us

104

grows toward wholehearted commitment to edifying one another that we approach "the measure of the stature of the fullness of Christ," the state of maturity to which the Lord is calling us. To the extent that we are conscious of and yielded to this truth, the Church experiences blessing, fruitfulness and growth.

It is crucial that Christians understand that every one of us is called to build. We all have the responsibility to help edify the Church. There are no exceptions, anywhere, in the entire Kingdom of God. We are each of us gifted, in varying ways, to edify the Body in love. To the extent we acknowledge our responsibility and exercise our gifts, to that extent we will strengthen and bless the Body and please the Lord. And to that extent we will have matured in Christ.

Here are some passages which clearly convey our charge to build and be built together with Christ. Note, in the first quote, the importance of building with carefulness, and the range of "build quality" grades, from precious gold to worthless straw, to be revealed one day by fire:

By the grace God has given me, I laid a foundation as an expert builder, and someone else is building on it. But each one should be careful how he builds. For no one can lay any foundation other than the one already laid, which is Jesus Christ. If any man builds on this foundation using gold, silver, costly stones, wood, hay or straw, his work will be shown for what it is, because the Day will bring it to light. It will be revealed with fire, and the fire will test the quality of each man's work. If what he has built survives, he will receive his reward. If it is burned up, he will suffer loss; he himself will be saved, but only as one escaping through the flames (1 Cor. 3 10 – 15).

So it is with you. Since you are eager to have spiritual gifts, try to excel in gifts that build up the church (1 Corinthians 14:12).

Each of us should please his neighbour for his good, to build him up (Romans 15:2).

Let us therefore make every effort to do what leads to peace and to mutual edification (Romans 19:19).

It was He who gave some to be apostles, some to be prophets, some to be evangelists, and some to be pastors and teachers, to prepare God's people for works of service, so that the body of Christ may be built up until we all reach unity in the faith and in the knowledge of the Son of God and become mature, attaining to the whole measure of the fullness of Christ. Then we will no longer be infants, tossed back and forth by the waves, and blown here and there by every wind of teaching and by the cunning and craftiness of men in their deceitful scheming. Instead, speaking the truth in love, we will grow to become in every respect the mature body of him who is the head, that is, Christ. From Him the whole body, joined and held together by every supporting ligament, grows and builds itself up in love, as each part does its work (Ephesians 4:11-16).

So then, just as you received Christ Jesus as Lord, continue to live in Him, rooted and built up in Him, strengthened in the faith as you were taught, and overflowing with thankfulness (Colossians 2:6-8).

He died for us so that, whether we are awake or asleep, we may live together with Him. Therefore encourage one another and build each other up, just as in fact you are doing (1 Thess 5:10-11).

We have all been called and gifted to edify the Body. Our gifts may differ, but we have one thing in common: the capacity and responsibility to pray. Biblical prayer is the mighty, unstoppable mountain-mover in the great work of edification. However hard the circumstances or daunting the challenges, all can pray. And, however prodigious one's gifting or abilities, none can truly succeed in ministry without prayer.

Each of us, whatever our calling or ministry, has the privilege and responsibility of seeking the Lord and lifting the Body up before Him at His throne of grace.

31. "Build the house, that I may be glorified," Says the Lord

Many believers who have lived through a church construction, expansion or renovation project have heard sermons and exhortations drawn from Haggai, a prophet in the time of Israel's restoration following the Babylonian captivity. Here's how the Book of Haggai begins:

In the second year of Darius the king, in the sixth month, on the first day of the month, the word of the Lord came by the hand of Haggai the prophet to Zerubbabel the son of Shealtiel, governor of Judah, and to Joshua the son of Jehozadak, the high priest: "Thus says the Lord of hosts: These people say the time has not yet come to rebuild the house of the Lord." Then the word of the Lord came by the hand of Haggai the prophet, "Is it a time for you yourselves to dwell in your paneled houses, while this house lies in ruins? Now, therefore, thus says the Lord of hosts: Consider your ways. You have sown much, and harvested little. You eat, but you never have enough; you drink, but you never have your fill. You clothe yourselves, but no one is warm. And he who earns wages does so to put them into a bag with holes."

"Thus says the Lord of hosts: Consider your ways. Go up to the hills and bring wood and build the house, that I may take pleasure in it and that I may be glorified, says the Lord. You looked for much, and behold, it came to little, And when you brought it home, I blew it away. Why? declares the Lord of hosts. Because of my house that lies in ruins, while each of you busies himself with his

own house. Therefore the heavens above you have withheld the dew, and the earth has withheld its produce. And I have called for a drought on the land and the hills, on the grain, the new wine, the oil, on what the ground brings forth, on man and beast, and on all their labours (Haggai 1:1-11).

Does this passage ring any bells? The typical application in the modern context is that believers have a responsibility to contribute to the construction or the upkeep of house of the Lord (i.e. the church building). Fail to give and you will lose, so pony up!

Applying the prophecy of Haggai in this way is not necessarily wrong. Believers in local churches do have a financial responsibility to help support and maintain the church, its facilities, its ministers and its programs. To take benefit from a church without contributing to its needs is simply wrong and displeases the Lord. Of course, churches that are totally preoccupied with their buildings are missing the will of God, but that's another discussion.

In any case, there is a far more appropriate and needful application of Haggai's prophetic message for believers today. We know that no church building can actually be "the house of the Lord." As Stephen told the Jewish leaders before they stoned him, "the Most High does not dwell in houses made by hands" (Acts 7:48). Church buildings are simply meeting places.

The true house of the Lord is the Body of Christ, the household of faith: "So then you are no longer strangers and aliens, but you are fellow citizens with the saints and members of the household of God, built on the foundation of the apostles and prophets, Christ Jesus himself being the cornerstone, in whom the whole structure, being joined together, grows into a holy temple in the Lord. In him you also are being built together into a dwelling place for God by the Spirit" (Eph. 2:19-22).

We, the saints of God, are the temple of the Lord. We have been joined together in Christ and are being built together, or edified, into a "place" for Him to dwell by His Spirit. Note that this building together is a process occurring over time, with a definite end in view: We need continually to be built up "until we all attain to the unity of the faith and of the knowledge of the Son of God, to mature manhood, to the measure of the stature of the fullness of Christ" (Eph. 4:13). And it is a process toward which all believers have gifting and responsibility to contribute.

Believers may tend, however, to seriously underestimate the importance to God of the health and integrity of His spiritual dwelling place, His Body. It's easy for us to sit back and observe, with rueful detachment, "That there's a mess . . . Oh, that's a pity, Christians blowing it again . . . More scandal . . . Another church split . . . Everything going down the tubes . . . Ho, hum."

Or, worse, believers may actually turn against the Church in their hearts, angry because it isn't what they know it ought to be. They grind their critical axes without ever lifting a finger, or a prayer, to strengthen and edify God's people.

God cannot be pleased with these attitudes. Jesus gave His life to redeem and cleanse His Bride, and would have us learn to love her the way He does. No matter how much apostasy and falling away there may be, He will have a glorious faithful remnant, and we are called to seek her blessing and victory.

So, going back to Haggai and his rather strong rebuke of the Jews who had either remained in the land or returned to it from Babylon: They had been devoting their time, attention and energy to restoring and building their own properties, homes and farms. Meanwhile, the Temple of God in Jerusalem lay in ruins. The people had calculated that looking after themselves was the first order of business and that the Temple could be restored some other time.

Consequently, God was displeased and had withheld blessing from them. The little they were able to produce, He "blew away." There was never enough food or drink or clothing or other necessities of life.

What those ancient Jews had done was to invert an enduring spiritual principle in pursuit of what they mistakenly thought would be their own gain. Centuries later, Jesus would clearly state this principle when He said, "Seek first the kingdom of God and His righteousness, and all these things will be added unto you" (Matt. 6:33). Those Jews were seeking first "all these things." As a result, they were missing out not only spiritually, but materially as well.

How might this episode in Jewish history apply to us, beyond provoking us to give money to the church building fund? God's spiritual temple, the Church, may not be lying in ruins. But it faces enormous challenges and has great needs. God's will, as expressed through Jesus in John 17 and the full teaching of the New Testament, is to protect, sanctify, edify and unify us—and to fill us, His dwelling place, with all of His own fullness (Eph. 3:19). Ultimately, the Lord longs to gather us to Himself, that we may behold Him in all of His power and glory and delight in Him and worship Him forever. He would that we, also, eagerly anticipate that blessed day and ready ourselves for it.

God has ordained that each member of His Body, both as individuals and in congregations, do its part to edify the whole Body in love. We are to help build up His dwelling place the Church, in order to honour and glorify Jesus, manifesting His truth, love and wisdom before the world and the rulers and authorities in the heavenly places (Eph. 3:10). The simple, vital question that both individuals and congregations in the Body of Christ must face, from the least to the greatest, is: Are we doing this? Are we seeking first the Kingdom of God and His righteousness? Are we aligning our priorities with the Lord's? Or are we seeking other things first, leaving the edification of the Body for another day or for someone else to do?

In response to Haggai's words, the leaders and the people feared the Lord. And the Lord said, through Haggai, "'I am with you' . . . And they came and worked on the house of the Lord of hosts, their God" (Haggai 1:13-14). "And the Lord said, 'Be strong, all you people of the land, declares the Lord. Work, for I am with you, declares the Lord of hosts, according to the covenant that I made with you when you came out of Egypt. My Spirit remains in your midst. Fear not. . . . I will fill this house with glory . . . The latter glory of this house shall be greater than the former, says the Lord of hosts. And in this place I will give peace, declares the Lord of hosts'" (Haggai 2:4-9).

What tremendous encouragement and promises God gave in response to the willing dedication of the ancient Jews to restoring the earthly temple of a fading dispensation: "Be strong . . . I am with you . . . my Spirit remains in your midst . . . fear not . . . I will fill this house with glory . . . in this place I will give peace."

How much better are God's encouragement and promises to His Church. And how much more—how very much more—He will bless us as we "seek first" to edify His true, spiritual temple, the Body of Christ, that He may dwell with us in His fullness and be glorified in us.

32. Why We Must Pray

God often chooses to accomplish His good purposes through human agency. He works through human teachers to impart His truth. He works through believers to manifest, through good deeds, His love and kindness to the world. And He works through biblical, loving, faith-filled, persistent prayer to bring eternal blessing both to those being prayed for, and to those who pray.

God's will is that His people love one another, and that we earnestly desire to see one another run the race well and finish it in victory. In His perfect wisdom, He has ordained that our effectual prayer for one another be a mighty incubator and generator of growth and of love—wise, discerning, edifying love.

The need for effectual, edifying prayer has perhaps never been greater. On one hand, God's people are facing unprecedented external perils and pressures, all over the world. Within the Church there is much apathy, worldliness, error and even apostasy. On the other hand, the Church has an irrevocable calling from God to rise up and fulfill. The Body of Christ must be equipped and built up "until we all attain to the unity of the faith and of the knowledge of the Son of God, to mature manhood, to the measure of the stature of the fullness of Christ" (Eph. 4:13).

That word "until" means that the process of building the Church has a definite direction and a definite end-state. Have we reached that end-state of mature manhood, the stature of the fullness of Christ? Hardly. Does this mean we can never reach it or that we ought not to reach for it? Certainly not.

If we wish to please God, we must believe His Word and obey His will concerning His Church, which is this: "We are to grow up in every way into him who is the head, into Christ, from whom the whole body, joined and held together by every joint with which it is

113

equipped, when each part is working properly, makes the body grow so that it builds itself up in love" (Eph. 4:15-16).

God's desire and plan is that the Body, through its connection to Christ, make itself grow up even more into Christ, unto the very "stature of the fullness of Christ." That is a high calling, and all of God's people have a part to play in fulfilling it. The Body grows when "each part is working properly." Every member has a responsibility to help edify the whole.

Surely, effectual prayer is an essential part of every believer's calling to edify the Body in love. Whether one is at present praying effectually or not, we are all called to pray. Prayer is not "everything," but effectual prayer is essential. The full blessing of the Lord, which is more than we can ask or even imagine, cannot be ours if we do not desire it and if we do not express our desire for it. The Church will not attain to maturity and victory without effectual, fervent, sustained, loving, scriptural prayer.

So, in this hour a great calling lies before the people of God, and great challenges—giants, some might call them—impede the way forward. But we must go forward, knowing that Jesus is building—not "may be building"—His Church, and knowing that His Body will be—not "may be"—built up in love until it comes to maturity.

The obstacles are numerous and great, but the power of God is greater. Jesus has promised to build His Church, and He is doing so. He will guide His people through all circumstances, and even use adversity to help accomplish His glorious purposes. In the deepening darkness of this present world, our light will grow brighter and brighter, to the glory of God. Surely His word to Israel applies no less to the Church of Jesus Christ: "See, darkness covers the earth and thick darkness is over the peoples, but the LORD rises upon you and his glory appears over you" (Isaiah 60:2).

The Lord's intention—His will—is that we edify one another in love until His Body comes to mature completeness in Him. This doesn't mean ignoring problems in the Church or failing to confront sin and error. It does mean continually praying with love and understanding for those who belong to Christ, that whatever the need may be, God will supply it.

As we pray effectually, we will help others who may be struggling. There are many a bruised reed and smoking flax among us who, thanks in part to loving and edifying prayer, will stand at the last in glorious victory. And in that day, the joy of those who upheld such and helped them to stand will be unspeakable and full of glory!

Effectual, fervent prayer is something of a mystery. After all, God does not need our help to do anything. He does not need to hear our prayer before He can strengthen believers by His Spirit in the inner man, or cause their love to abound, or fill them with the knowledge of His will in all spiritual wisdom and understanding. God can, and does, do these things freely when and as He determines. Yet He has constrained Himself, to some extent, by granting His bestowal of blessings in response to our effectual, fervent prayer. On one hand, Jesus said, "Ask, and you will receive," and on the other said, "You have not because you ask not."

I believe a very big part of the answer to the mystery of prayer is this: When we pray according to God's will (that is, according to His word), we who pray are transformed. Our hearts are enlarged, both toward the Lord and His word and His will, and toward the people for whom we pray. As we pray biblically, we grow—in understanding, in faith, in love, in thankfulness, and in every good thing. Labouring in biblical prayer brings forth blessings and growth in those who pray which, apparently, cannot be obtained in any other manner.

My conviction is that, perhaps above all, biblical prayer teaches and encourages and empowers us to love others. It opens our hearts to the deeply challenging command of Jesus in John 15, that we love one another. Through biblical prayer, as we hold others up and seek their good before God's throne of grace, we find the God-given means to transcend our human weakness and incapacity to love. Through biblical prayer, we can truly begin to love those whom, in our frail humanity, we simply "cannot" love, or love insufficiently.

Furthermore, in praying earnestly for the Church, according to the clear teaching of Scripture, we begin to understand and even to abound in the self-sacrificial love Christ has for His bride. We begin to realize that as Jesus loves her, so should we and so can we. Every believer has an important role to play building her up and preparing her for glory: "Hallelujah! For our Lord God Almighty reigns. Let us rejoice and be glad and give him glory! For the wedding of the Lamb has come, and his bride has made herself ready" (Revelation 19:6-7). Are you ready to help the bride of Christ make herself ready?

Through biblical prayer, we gain a deep and vital interest in the eternal rejoicing of our brothers and sisters. Jesus has commissioned every disciple to labour together with Him in His Father's business. He has disclosed His glorious plans and purposes to us as to friends, and invites us to take up the yoke and share the burden He unveils to us in John 17. Perfect in wisdom, the Lord does all things well. Part of His delight in our ultimate union with Him will be to see our rejoicing in the triumph of those for whom we have sought, through prayer, victory over the world, the flesh and the devil.

As all believers are well aware, the Church is facing immense challenges in this hour. These challenges will compel us to grow up into Christ, as that is the only way that we can face them. Through it all, the Lord is preparing us to display to the world and its ruling principalities and powers the fullness of maturity and blessedness that He has promised to bring forth, and is well able to bring forth, in His people.

The Church is in need of loving, edifying prayer. Enormous mountains stand between us and "mature manhood, the measure of the stature of the fullness of Christ" (Eph. 4:13). God has glorious things in mind for His people, but, as with the ancient Israelites and their inheritance, we must, in His power, contend for them. We need to turn to Him with our whole hearts and desire what He desires for us.

I believe God is calling, stirring and raising up believers to seek Him and the fulfillment of His will, according to His Word. The task is daunting, but it is not impossible. As for those mountains, we can take heart from the prophecy of Zechariah to Zerubbabel, who was commissioned with restoring Jerusalem and the Temple following the Babylonian captivity. Jerusalem at the time was a very sad, sorry scene. Nevertheless, God had a plan and, through Zechariah, gave a word:

> This is what the LORD says to Zerubbabel: "It is not by force nor by strength, but by my Spirit, says the LORD of Heaven's Armies. Nothing, not even a mighty mountain, will stand in Zerubbabel's way; it will become a level plain before him! And when Zerubbabel sets the final stone of the Temple in place, the people will shout: 'May God bless it! May God bless it!'" Then another message came to me from the LORD: "Zerubbabel is the one who laid the foundation of this Temple, and he will complete it. Then you will know that the LORD of Heaven's Armies has sent me. Do not despise these small beginnings, for the LORD rejoices to see the work begin, to see the plumb line in Zerubbabel's hand." (Zech. 4:6-10, NLT).

If you recognize that the Lord is calling you to seek Him for the good of His people, for the glory of His

117

Name, the best thing you can do is to simply begin to respond. Take a small step. It will lead to another. Begin to draw near to God, and He will draw near to you. Do not focus on the "impossible" mountains, but look to Him for whom nothing is impossible, least of all that which He has promised. Yes, we may be small and weak. But let us not "despise the day of small beginnings." The Lord has a plan. And He has given to us, also, a sure word.

Hebrews 10:24 says, "Let us think of ways to motivate one another to acts of love and good works." May this little volume help motivate you to love and to the good work of edifying prayer.

Appendix: Prayer Passages in Paul's Epistles

What follows is a compilation, in order of place in the Bible, of virtually all of the passages in Paul's epistles in which the apostle either states what he is praying for, or teaches and exhorts on prayer, or requests prayer for himself. Receptive meditation on these passages will bring insight, fruitfulness and delight to any believer's prayer life.

These verses reveal the will of God for His people, the attitude and heart with which we ought to pray for the saints, and the things for which we can and should ask the Father, with full confidence, at His throne of grace. By following Paul's example and teaching on prayer, any believer will help to edify the Body of Christ, will greatly please the Lord, and will be blessed now and in eternity.

Rom. 1:8-12
8 First, I thank my God through Jesus Christ for all of you, because your faith is being reported all over the world.
9 God, whom I serve with my whole heart in preaching the gospel of his Son, is my witness how constantly I remember you
10 in my prayers at all times; and I pray that now at last by God's will the way may be opened for me to come to you.
11 I long to see you so that I may impart to you some spiritual gift to make you strong–
12 that is, that you and I may be mutually encouraged by each other's faith.

Rom. 10:1
1 Brothers, my heart's desire and prayer to God for the Israelites is that they may be saved.

Rom. 15:5-6

5 May the God who gives endurance and encouragement give you a spirit of unity among yourselves as you follow Christ Jesus,

6 so that with one heart and mouth you may glorify the God and Father of our Lord Jesus Christ.

Rom. 15:13

13 May the God of hope fill you with all joy and peace as you trust in him, so that you may overflow with hope by the power of the Holy Spirit.

Rom. 15:30-33

30 I urge you, brothers, by our Lord Jesus Christ and by the love of the Spirit, to join me in my struggle by praying to God for me.

31 Pray that I may be rescued from the unbelievers in Judea and that my service in Jerusalem may be acceptable to the saints there,

32 so that by God's will I may come to you with joy and together with you be refreshed.

33 The God of peace be with you all. Amen.

2 Cor. 1:8-11

8 We do not want you to be uninformed, brothers and sisters, about the troubles we experienced in the province of Asia. We were under great pressure, far beyond our ability to endure, so that we despaired of life itself.

9 Indeed, we felt we had received the sentence of death. But this happened that we might not rely on ourselves but on God, who raises the dead.

10 He has delivered us from such a deadly peril, and he will deliver us again. On him we have set our hope that he will continue to deliver us,

11 as you help us by your prayers. Then many will give thanks on our behalf for the gracious favor granted us in answer to the prayers of many.

2 Cor. 13:7

7 Now we pray to God that you will not do anything wrong. Not that people will see that we have stood the test but that you will do what is right even though we may seem to have failed.

2 Cor. 13:9

9 We are glad whenever we are weak but you are strong; and our prayer is for your perfection.

Eph. 1:15-23

15 For this reason, ever since I heard about your faith in the Lord Jesus and your love for all the saints,

16 I have not stopped giving thanks for you, remembering you in my prayers.

17 I keep asking that the God of our Lord Jesus Christ, the glorious Father, may give you the Spirit of wisdom and revelation, so that you may know him better.

18 I pray also that the eyes of your heart may be enlightened in order that you may know the hope to which he has called you, the riches of his glorious inheritance in the saints,

19 and his incomparably great power for us who believe. That power is like the working of his mighty strength,

20 which he exerted in Christ when he raised him from the dead and seated him at his right hand in the heavenly realms,

21 far above all rule and authority, power and dominion, and every title that can be given, not only in the present age but also in the one to come.

22 And God placed all things under his feet and appointed him to be head over everything for the church,

23 which is his body, the fullness of him who fills everything in every way.

Eph. 3:14-21

14 For this reason I kneel before the Father,

15 from whom his whole family in heaven and on earth derives its name.

16 I pray that out of his glorious riches he may strengthen you with power through his Spirit in your inner being,

17 so that Christ may dwell in your hearts through faith. And I pray that you, being rooted and established in love,

18 may have power, together with all the saints, to grasp how wide and long and high and deep is the love of Christ,

19 and to know this love that surpasses knowledge— that you may be filled to the measure of all the fullness of God.

20 Now to him who is able to do immeasurably more than all we ask or imagine, according to his power that is at work within us,

21 to him be glory in the church and in Christ Jesus throughout all generations, for ever and ever! Amen.

Eph. 6:17-20

17 Take the helmet of salvation and the sword of the Spirit, which is the word of God.

18 And pray in the Spirit on all occasions with all kinds of prayers and requests. With this in mind, be alert and always keep on praying for all the saints.

19 Pray also for me, that whenever I open my mouth, words may be given me so that I will fearlessly make known the mystery of the gospel,

20 for which I am an ambassador in chains. Pray that I may declare it fearlessly, as I should.

Phil. 1:1-11

1 Paul and Timothy, servants of Christ Jesus, To all the saints in Christ Jesus at Philippi, together with the overseers and deacons:

2 Grace and peace to you from God our Father and the Lord Jesus Christ.

3 I thank my God every time I remember you.

4 In all my prayers for all of you, I always pray with joy

5 because of your partnership in the gospel from the first day until now,

6 being confident of this, that he who began a good work in you will carry it on to completion until the day of Christ Jesus.

7 It is right for me to feel this way about all of you, since I have you in my heart; for whether I am in chains or defending and confirming the gospel, all of you share in God's grace with me.

8 God can testify how I long for all of you with the affection of Christ Jesus.

9 And this is my prayer: that your love may abound more and more in knowledge and depth of insight,

10 so that you may be able to discern what is best and may be pure and blameless until the day of Christ,

11 filled with the fruit of righteousness that comes through Jesus Christ—to the glory and praise of God.

Phil. 1:18-19
18 Yes, and I will continue to rejoice,

19 for I know that through your prayers and God's provision of the Spirit of Jesus Christ what has happened to me will turn out for my deliverance.

Phil. 4:6-7
6 Do not be anxious about anything, but in everything, by prayer and petition, with thanksgiving, present your requests to God.

7 And the peace of God, which transcends all understanding, will guard your hearts and your minds in Christ Jesus.

Col. 1:3-12
3 We always thank God, the Father of our Lord Jesus Christ, when we pray for you,

4 because we have heard of your faith in Christ Jesus and of the love you have for all the saints—

5 the faith and love that spring from the hope that is stored up for you in heaven and that you have already heard about in the word of truth, the gospel

6 that has come to you. All over the world this gospel is bearing fruit and growing, just as it has been doing

among you since the day you heard it and understood God's grace in all its truth.

7 You learned it from Epaphras, our dear fellow servant, who is a faithful minister of Christ on our behalf,

8 and who also told us of your love in the Spirit.

9 For this reason, since the day we heard about you, we have not stopped praying for you and asking God to fill you with the knowledge of his will through all spiritual wisdom and understanding.

10 And we pray this in order that you may live a life worthy of the Lord and may please him in every way: bearing fruit in every good work, growing in the knowledge of God,

11 being strengthened with all power according to his glorious might so that you may have great endurance and patience, and joyfully

12 giving thanks to the Father, who has qualified you to share in the inheritance of the saints in the kingdom of light.

Col. 2:1-3

1 I want you to know how much I am struggling for you and for those at Laodicea, and for all who have not met me personally.

2 My purpose is that they may be encouraged in heart and united in love, so that they may have the full riches of complete understanding, in order that they may know the mystery of God, namely, Christ,

3 in whom are hidden all the treasures of wisdom and knowledge.

Col. 4:2-4

2 Devote yourselves to prayer, being watchful and thankful.

3 And pray for us, too, that God may open a door for our message, so that we may proclaim the mystery of Christ, for which I am in chains.

4 Pray that I may proclaim it clearly, as I should.

Col. 4:12-13

12 Epaphras, who is one of you and a servant of Christ Jesus, sends greetings. He is always wrestling in prayer for you, that you may stand firm in all the will of God, mature and fully assured.

13 I vouch for him that he is working hard for you and for those at Laodicea and Hierapolis.

1 Thess. 3:9-13

9 How can we thank God enough for you in return for all the joy we have in the presence of our God because of you?

10 Night and day we pray most earnestly that we may see you again and supply what is lacking in your faith.

11 Now may our God and Father himself and our Lord Jesus clear the way for us to come to you.

12 May the Lord make your love increase and overflow for each other and for everyone else, just as ours does for you.

13 May he strengthen your hearts so that you will be blameless and holy in the presence of our God and Father when our Lord Jesus comes with all his holy ones.

1 Thess. 5:16-18

16 Be joyful always;

17 pray continually;

18 give thanks in all circumstances, for this is God's will for you in Christ Jesus.

1 Thess. 5:23-25

23 May God himself, the God of peace, sanctify you through and through. May your whole spirit, soul and body be kept blameless at the coming of our Lord Jesus Christ.

24 The one who calls you is faithful and he will do it.

25 Brothers, pray for us.

2 Thess. 1:11-12

11 With this in mind, we constantly pray for you, that our God may count you worthy of his calling, and that

by his power he may fulfill every good purpose of yours and every act prompted by your faith.

12 We pray this so that the name of our Lord Jesus may be glorified in you, and you in him, according to the grace of our God and the Lord Jesus Christ.

2 Thess. 2:16-17

16 May our Lord Jesus Christ himself and God our Father, who loved us and by his grace gave us eternal encouragement and good hope,

17 encourage your hearts and strengthen you in every good deed and word.

2 Thess. 3:1-2

1 Finally, brothers, pray for us that the message of the Lord may spread rapidly and be honored, just as it was with you.

2 And pray that we may be delivered from wicked and evil men, for not everyone has faith.

2 Thess. 3:16

16 Now may the Lord of peace himself give you peace at all times and in every way. The Lord be with all of you.

1 Tim. 2:1-4

1 I urge, then, first of all, that requests, prayers, intercession and thanksgiving be made for everyone—

2 for kings and all those in authority, that we may live peaceful and quiet lives in all godliness and holiness.

3 This is good, and pleases God our Savior,

4 who wants all men to be saved and to come to a knowledge of the truth.

1 Tim. 2:8

8 I want men everywhere to lift up holy hands in prayer, without anger or disputing.

2 Tim. 1:3-4

3 I thank God, whom I serve, as my forefathers did, with a clear conscience, as night and day I constantly remember you in my prayers.

4 Recalling your tears, I long to see you, so that I may be filled with joy.

Philemon 1:4-6
4 I always thank my God as I remember you in my prayers,
5 because I hear about your faith in the Lord Jesus and your love for all the saints.
6 I pray that you may be active in sharing your faith, so that you will have a full understanding of every good thing we have in Christ.

Hebrews 4:14-16 (assuming Paul wrote this epistle)
14 Therefore, since we have a great high priest who has ascended into heaven, Jesus the Son of God, let us hold firmly to the faith we profess.
15 For we do not have a high priest who is unable to empathize with our weaknesses, but we have one who has been tempted in every way, just as we are—yet he did not sin.
16 Let us then approach God's throne of grace with confidence, so that we may receive mercy and find grace to help us in our time of need.

Hebrews 13:18-21
18 Pray for us. We are sure that we have a clear conscience and desire to live honorably in every way.
19 I particularly urge you to pray so that I may be restored to you soon.
20 May the God of peace, who through the blood of the eternal covenant brought back from the dead our Lord Jesus, that great Shepherd of the sheep,
21 equip you with everything good for doing his will, and may he work in us what is pleasing to him, through Jesus Christ, to whom be glory for ever and ever. Amen.

Contact the author: jdryan@telus.net

Made in the USA
Middletown, DE
21 April 2022

64573781R10076